**"Remember, you are not here to enjoy the trappings of power but to do a job and to uphold the highest standards in public life"**
Tony Blair, May 1997

**"I think that most people who have dealt with me think that I am a pretty straight sort of guy – and I am"**
Tony Blair, November 1997, *On The Record*

**"Their politics without conscience brought fascination to begin with, then admiration; next it will bring disillusion; finally, it will bring contempt"**
William Hague, October 1997

D0495424

# The Little Red Book of
# New Labour
# Sleaze

Edited by
Iain Dale
and Guido Fawkes

## Written by bloggers

Politico's Media

First published in Great Britain 2006
by Politico's Media
PO BOX 279, Tunbridge Wells, Kent, TN2 4WJ

A catalogue record for this book is available from the British Library.

ISBN 1904734162
Printed and bound in Great Britain by CGI Europe

# Contents

## New Labour Sleaze in . . . 2006    129

## And Also. . .    149

## STOP PRESS

## Useful Links      **177**

MY GOVERNMENT
WILL BE
WHITER THAN
WHITE

# Iain's Introduction

The last week of April 2006 saw the political equivalent of a 'Perfect Storm'. Patricia Hewitt was booed by nurses, Charles Clarke was in trouble over foreign prisoners who had not been deported, John Prescott had been exposed for bonking his cocktail sausage-eating diary secretary and in the most bizarre twist of all, cannabis was found in the home of the Defence Secretary, Dr John Reid. This followed a month of dire publicity for New Labour over cash for peerages. Could it get worse for Tony Blair? Yes. Guido Fawkes and I announced the publication of this book.

My fellow blogger Guido Fawkes emailed me on the evening of 30th April to suggest writing this book. The idea immediately appealed but we needed to catch the wave of the rising tide of scandals that were threatening to engulf Tony Blair. So we decided to ask our friends in the world of political blogdom to help us write the book. The response was terrific and the book was printed and in the bookshops within three weeks of Guido first coming up with the idea. Phew! It's the first time a book has been written entirely by bloggers.

I'd like to thank Beau Bo D'Or (www.bbdo.co.uk/blog) for designing the front cover and Hoby (www.hobycartoons.com) for the cartoons. Thanks also to Barry Arrowsmith for his research and to Olly Figg for proofing the book in double-quick time.

There is a website to accompany the book at www.newlaboursleaze.com but do please visit my daily blog of political gossip, insight and humour at www.iaindale.blogspot.com

This book is deliberately inconsistent both in writing style and content. It couldn't be anything else with around 70 contributors. We hope you enjoy it.

*Iain Dale*
*Tunbridge Wells, May 2006*

# Guido's Introduction

As another wave of New Labour sleaze washed up over the rotting body politic like yesterday's sewage, Tony Blair again made another attempt to make out that it was not as bad as the bad old Tory days. But it is worse I thought. At least the Tories didn't get up to hanky-panky on government premises, in government time at our expense with the taxpayer getting screwed as well as the semi-naked civil servant. Someone should really document it all so that the next time Tony claimed he was a "straight sorta guy" they would have the evidence to prove him wrong.

Intoxicated with that idea I emailed Iain Dale, knowing he had been keeping a close eye on developments and knows a thing or two about books. The next morning he replied with a publishing timetable. It was his idea to garner the British political blogosphere into co-authoring it quickly to catch the zeitgeist. This book introduces a wealth of diverse new writers to the book-reading public, as for most of our blogging co-authors this is the first time they have been in print on paper as opposed to pixels on screen.

We have calculated that over nine years New Labour has produced a scandal a month on average, with little time off for good behaviour. Nevertheless within these pages we document everything; shady bungs from businessmen, lying lobbyists, ministers on the make, expenses fiddled and loans for lordships made. So next time Tony Blair stands up to say New Labour is "whiter than white", you can throw this little red book at him.

*Guido Fawkes*
*Co Wexford, Ireland, May 2006*

# New Labour Sleaze in . . .

# 1997

## Tony's Sleazeometer, 1997

5 sleazy episodes: Not Very Straight Guy

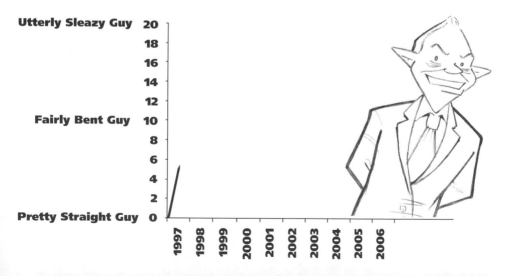

| | |
|---|---|
| **Utterly Sleazy Guy** | 20 |
| | 18 |
| | 16 |
| | 14 |
| | 12 |
| **Fairly Bent Guy** | 10 |
| | 8 |
| | 6 |
| | 4 |
| | 2 |
| **Pretty Straight Guy** | 0 |

1997 1998 1999 2000 2001 2002 2003 2004 2005 2006

# Straight Sorta Guy

## Dominic Llewellyn

In March 1997, a month before Tony Blair and Labour were elected to power, the future Prime Minister said, "We have got to be whiter than white if we are to rebuild trust in government." However, two months earlier, Labour had accepted a £1 million donation from one of the richest men in Britain, Formula One supremo Bernie Ecclestone. Labour, in both their 1992 and 1997 manifestos, had pledged to ban tobacco advertising. Once in power they published proposals to ban it from sports events from the end of 2003, with an exemption for Formula One for whom the ban would begin in 2006. The aforementioned Mr Ecclestone just so happened to be the owner of the rights to Formula One.

WHITER THAN WH...

After much pressure Labour were forced to hand the money back with Tony Blair granting a hastily arranged interview to John Humphreys on *On the Record*, saying, "I think I'm a pretty straight sorta guy." Andrew Rawnsley of the *Observer*, writing in his book *Servants of the People*, claimed that Gordon Brown lied when telling Radio 4's *Today* he knew nothing about the donation. Brown admitted the lie privately afterwards by saying "If this gets out, I'll be destroyed". Rawnsley also stated that Blair claimed he had sought advice about the £1 million donation from Lord Neill, chairman of the Committee on Standards in Public Life, before any journalists had been in touch. According to Rawnsley, however, in fact the Prime Minister contacted Lord Neill only after reporters began to break the scandal. And his letter asked for advice about a possible second donation, not the first. William Hague, the then leader of the Conservative Party said, "No more serious allegation has been made against a sitting prime minister in modern times."

Guess who Bernie Ecclestone's lawyer was? Step forward David Mills, husband of Labour Minister Tessa Jowell and himself to become embroiled in scandal eight years later.

Although Labour returned the cash to Ecclestone, it is now alleged that Labour asked him to delay cashing the cheque to avert a cashflow crisis. It is thought that it took up to nine months for the cheque to be fully redeemed.

# Fiona Jones's Election Expenses

Daniel Harvey

Controversy marred the election of Fiona Jones as Member of Parliament for Newark in 1997. Labour won the seat with a majority of 3,016 votes, but within weeks of the General Election on 1st May, an investigation was launched into how much was spent during the campaign, and whether it breached the spending limits.

The row began when Labour submitted their expenses for the election campaign. Liberal Democrat candidate Peter Harris said, "Frankly I find it hard to credit that Labour spent less that £60 a week running an office at a prime Newark town centre site during a six-week campaign. It is an astonishingly low figure."

By December 1997 officers from the Nottinghamshire Police Fraud Squad had began an investigation into the allegations, and on 12th March 1998 Fiona Jones was interviewed by the police.

Having been found guilty at the resulting court case in March 1999, she automatically lost her seat and was ordered to complete 100 hours' community service.

At the subsequent appeal on 15th April 1999 Jones had her appeal against conviction for election fraud upheld. After a High Court ruling sought by Speaker of the House of Commons Betty Boothroyd to clarify matters as a result of the successful appeal by Mrs Jones, the way was cleared for her return to the House of Commons. The Speaker told the House: "The Newark seat is not vacant."

A motion welcoming her back was signed by 34 MPs. But the damage to Fiona's reputation was done.

At the following general election in June 2001 the Conservative Party regained the seat with a majority of 4,000 and a huge swing of 7.5%.

# A Choice of Diary Secretaries

Iain Dale

John Prescott wasn't the first Labour Cabinet minister to have an affair with his diary secretary. Robin Cook not only had an affair with his constituency diary secretary, he tried to procure her the same job in the Foreign Office. The only trouble was that the incumbent didn't want to shift. Anne Bullen, the then Foreign Secretary's diary secretary was a formidable woman and was not to be trifled with. But she was on a fixed-term contract which finished in June 1997. In a written answer to Parliament Robin Cook said, "Miss Anne Bullen was informed that I had decided that her fixed-term contract should not be renewed, and that she should be replaced. She was informed that Ms Gaynor Regan was being considered for the post of Diary Secretary. She was also informed when, shortly thereafter, I decided that she should not take up the position." In a separate answer he said: "Gaynor Regan had been employed as my diary secretary for four years in opposition and had worked well in the post. She was therefore an obvious candidate for the appointment, but I reached my own conclusion that, in view of our relationship, it would not be right to appoint her. I invited the Department to proceed with an internal appointment on 30 May." He never explained why he had Gaynor Regan's name withdrawn and described press reports that Miss Regan's appointment had actually been vetoed by MI5 and senior civil servants as "absolute fantasy".

The Foreign Secretary then did what most Labour politicians do in the circumstances. He attempted to trash Miss Bullen's reputation. At an EU summit he described her as "impossible to work with". Miss Bullen hit back. In a newspaper article, Miss Bullen is said to have told a friend, "It was quite wrong of the Secretary of State to ever contemplate getting rid of me so he could give his lover my job." She is also said to have dismissed a suggestion by Labour sources that she was a "card-carrying Conservative", apparently insisting, "I am not, and never have been, a member of the Tory Party." Former Foreign Office minister David Davis dismissed as "madness" the suggestion that Miss Bullen was "somehow some sort of closet Tory". He told BBC Radio 4's *World At One* programme: "I knew the lady for three years and hundreds of meetings. Never once did I hear her make a political comment of either persuasion or any persuasion."

*Iain Dale's Diary, www.iaindale.blogspot.com*

# New Labour Sleaze in . . .

# 1998

## Tony's Sleazeometer, 1998

9 sleazy episodes: Quite a Bent Guy

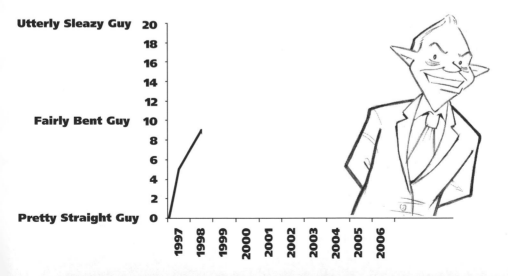

Utterly Sleazy Guy — 20, 18, 16, 14, 12

Fairly Bent Guy — 10, 8, 6, 4, 2

Pretty Straight Guy — 0

1997 1998 1999 2000 2001 2002 2003 2004 2005 2006

# Robin Cook's Balls

Michael Dixon

The late Robin Cook will quite rightly be best remembered as the only anti-war member of the Cabinet who had the balls to resign before the Iraq war actually began. But in August 1998 his 'spherical objects' managed to get him into a completely different sort of scrape, when he succeeded in becoming the first senior New Labour figure to become embroiled in a sex scandal.

Kept secret from everyone, excluding of course the all-knowing upper echelons of the Labour Party, who had known of the issue since well before the 1997 election, Cook was conducting an affair with his diary secretary, Gaynor Regan. But on Friday 1st August 1998, as Cook was about to jet off to Colorado on holiday with his wife, Margaret, Downing Street discovered the *News Of The World* was to splash with the story the following Sunday. They had film of Cook walking out of Gaynor's flat to feed a parking meter and looking rather furtive. Small wonder, it was Gaynor's car that was parked. En route to the airport with his wife Cook received a call from Alastair Campbell. "You're in the shit", he told him. "I can buy you a few hours." Cook, knowing he had to make a decision about the future of his marriage before the story broke, decided to stay with his mistress. Sitting Margaret down in the departure lounge, he coolly informed her that the holiday was off, and he was divorcing her. Understandably, his wife was less than amused, and hoping she could be dissuaded from causing too much fuss and bringing about any serious harm to the Government's reputation, Tony Blair personally sent her a note wishing her the best. But even a visit by a reluctant Peter Mandelson to her home in Edinburgh could not hold back her fury. She alleged Cook had a history of alcohol abuse, claiming he had collapsed in a hotel room in 1987 after polishing off a bottle of brandy, and had worked his way through six mistresses during their relationship. She succeeded in fuelling stories that covered the front pages for weeks, but were no doubt rather off-putting to most of the British public, who had previously been unable to distinguish the country's latest sex god from a garden gnome. Gaynor, the lucky girl, married her troll at a Tunbridge Wells registry office later that year.

# Lobbygate 1

Shaun Rolph

"I can have tea with Geoffrey Robinson, I can get into Ed Balls." It's June 1998, just over a year after New Labour's victory, and Derek Draper, former assistant to Peter Mandelson turned lobbyist, is boasting of his contacts to a potential client. But the client is really the investigative journalist and left-wing scalp-flasher Greg Palast. And he is about to get a lesson in what Draper calls, "Policy World – the little world of business people and politicians".

Draper tells how he bypassed the "useless" Margaret Beckett at the DTI and the "nobody going nowhere" Michael Meacher at Environment to bring one of his clients, Ed Wallis, the chairman of Powergen, directly to the Treasury to discuss a previously rejected merger between Powergen and East Midlands Electricity. Draper claims that now, after this meeting between Wallis and Geoffrey Robinson, that rejection "will not happen again". On 25th June, Powergen announces its intention to buy East Midlands Electricity, "subject to approval". Peter Mandelson replaces Margaret Beckett at the DTI on 27th July. One of his first acts is to approve Powergen's takeover.

Powergen were fortunate to need New Labour's help when New Labour needed them to save the coal industry by signing supply contracts. As another lobbyist, Ben Lucas of Lawson, Lucas, Mendelsohn, told Palast, "This government likes to do deals." LLM performed the "cultural reshaping" of their clients Tesco. This included Tesco giving £12 million to the Dome in February 1998. In July 1998 a proposed car-park tax that could have cost them £20 million was scrapped.

Another partner in LLM, Jon Mendelsohn, explained how New Labour's deals with business were not just tactical but were central to its strategy. He said, "Labour's super-majority... means the only countervailing force is the media and business. So when the economy turns soft... we will make certain they stay with us. If we have business and media, the people will come along."

They certainly had the media. No government minister was affected. Geoffrey Robinson and Peter Mandelson were to be involved in other scandals before they had to resign. Ed Balls is now an MP.

Only Derek Draper lost his job. He left politics and went to California to become a psychologist. Now married to a breakfast TV presenter and with a child, he can look back philosophically on his "idiot years". "My message was quite simple really, 'I'm rich and a bit of a wanker. Who cares? You can still be that and be Labour'."

# Mandelson's Mortgages and Geoffrey Robinson's Building Society

Guido Fawkes

Multi-millionaire Geoffrey Robinson's loan of £373,000 to Peter Mandelson for a Notting Hill flat was their mutual undoing. The Coventry North West MP was the Paymaster General. Secretary of State Peter Mandelson's department, the DTI, was investigating irregularities in Mr Robinson's business affairs, dating back to the late 1980s. Mandelson did not think it necessary to declare the loan, despite the obvious conflict of interest presented by an indebted minister investigating another member of the Government's affairs, when the person under investigation is also his main personal creditor. The loan itself was made in mysterious circumstances. Mandelson actually had two loans for the flat, a bank mortgage upon which he had sworn on the application that he had no other loans, as well as the additional loan from Geoffrey Robinson

In November 1998 pressure was already growing for Robinson to resign, as evidence of more shady dealings emerged. Robinson was censured by the Committee on Standards and Privileges for failing to register the fact that Stenbell Ltd – a company he owned shares in – acquired a rights issue of 9,805,550 shares in another company, TransTec, from him. Stenbell then sold the issue to the Orion Trust, of which Mr Robinson was a discretionary beneficiary. Tony Blair gave him his full unqualified support. He resigned the next month, just a few hours after Peter Mandelson. A pattern was first established with this double resignation, in which the Prime Minister's unconditional support is the precursor to the resignation of a New Labour minister.

It subsequently emerged that Robinson had lobbied for planning permission for a massive development associated with Coventry City FC, of which he was a major shareholder through an offshore trust. Transtec called in the receivers in January

2000, a mere nine years after Robinson had taken charge of the firm (before resigning when appointed Paymaster General).

Robinson, a close ally of Gordon Brown, was never afraid to use his wealth to further his influence in the Labour Party, going as far as buying the *New Statesman*. The ailing magazine became increasingly anti-Blair under his ownership. Many speculate that under a Brown premiership, Geoffrey Robinson's loyalty will be rewarded once again.

*www.order-order.com*

# Lobbygate 2

Guido Fawkes

Greg Palast was investigating the murky world of New Labour lobbying for the *Observer* newspaper when he met Derek Draper the former chief aide to Peter Mandelson. "Dolly" Draper claimed to have "special access" to the Treasury and Downing Street. Palast was pretending to be a potential client. Draper boasted openly of what he could do: "I can have tea with Geoffrey Robinson [the then Paymaster-General], I can get into Ed Balls [the Chancellor's then economic adviser now an MP]." All this would be available to a client paying the lobbyist's fees. Draper even boasted that he could get advance economic information. He claimed to have provided advance knowledge on government spending, information that would be crucial to government bond traders like Salomon Brothers, to whom he boasted he had leaked the data: "It's inside information... If they [Salomon Brothers] acted on it, they'd have made a fortune."

But Draper was just one of many New Labour insiders now peddling influence on an industrial scale in a way not seen since Lloyd George.

Lawson Lucas Mendelsohn (LLM) was set up by Blairite insider Neal Lawson, who advised Tony Blair on campaign strategy before the election; Ben Lucas, who conducted Blair's political briefings; and Jon Mendelsohn who handled the future Prime Minister's contacts with business. Lucas boasted to Palast that he too could get inside information about public spending: "intelligence which in market terms would be worth a lot of money". He could do better than Draper's access to Geoffrey Robinson, he could "reach anyone. We can go to Gordon Brown if we have to". His partner Lawson boasted that he could arrange lunch "in the Downing Street dining room, it's not difficult for me to take people into these people."

Was it idle boasting by fee-hungry lobbyists? No, the mentality of New Labour meant that government special advisors were often merely pausing their career before becoming lobbyists or MPs. They are integral to New Labour's influence-peddling money-go-round. Roger Liddle was Blair's European Special Advisor at the No 10 Policy Unit. A friend of Derek Draper, he described the influence-peddling money-go-round very well. He told the *Observer*'s undercover investigator "There is a Circle and Derek is part of The Circle. And anyone who says he isn't is An Enemy. Derek knows all the right people. Whenever you are ready, just tell me what you want, who you want to meet and Derek and I will make the call for you." Liddle, the PM's European Special Advisor at the time he said that, had been a lobbyist for Prima Europe. His shareholding in the firm was put in a 'blind trust' when he went to work in Downing Street. How blind he was to the interests of his clients is revealed by knowing that Derek Draper's firm bought his holding while he was still in Downing Street.

The influence of lobbyists like LLM borders on the outrageous. They rented out their contacts for clients who were encouraged to support politically sensitive projects in one area for favour in another area. Tesco got central government support for planning deregulation after it gave £12 million towards the doomed Millennium Dome as advised by LLM. LLM clients got gambling deregulated to their profit via private meetings behind closed doors arranged away from the prying eyes of the public. As with secret loans, New Labour likes its favoured lobbyists to do their dirty business in secret. Ladbrokes used LLM to lobby Tessa Jowell, the minister with responsibility for the gambling industry. It came as no surprise when it was revealed that Gideon Hoffman, the civil servant behind the controversial scheme to introduce Las Vegas-style super casinos, had secretly applied for a job with Ladbrokes' owners. Ladbrokes would only say that "Over several years, following the advent of the proposed Gambling Bill, there has been a great deal of active political lobbying between ourselves and government. It is part of the normal democratic lobbying process. We will not go into what were private meetings."

New Labour makes laws behind closed doors, drafted by lobbyists with friends in government who give each other jobs and pay each other consultancy fees. This is the sleazy world that they call "the normal democratic lobbying process".

*Footnote: Derek Draper is now a professional psychologist and is married to GMTV's Kate Garraway. Rodger Liddle is head of the office of the President of the European Commission. Neal Lawson has fallen out of love with New Labour and runs Compass, a leftish think tank.*

# Forced out of the Closet

Michael Lyons

On 7th November 1998, the *News Of the World* rang Downing Street to inform them of allegations made by a former lover of Agriculture Minister Nick Brown. The story would be published the following day and would centre on Nick Brown's use of a male prostitute – or in tabloid parlance, a 'rent boy'.

The government was already reeling somewhat from the suicide of closeted gay Labour MP Gordon McMaster, who cited an anti-gay smear campaign conducted by rival Labour MPs in his suicide note as the cause; a claim Nick Brown himself dismissed, despite one MP being suspended over the matter. The news that the Agriculture Minister was also about to be outed had to have been met with a cry of "Not again!" in Downing Street. After all, it was barely a month after the Welsh Secretary Ron Davies was mugged by a man he was seeking to have casual sex with on Clapham Common and, as a result, quickly forced to resign in order to prevent a press frenzy before the publication of Labour's "Family Bill". Nick Brown steadfastly denied ever paying money for sex. He admitted to bestowing a number of gifts "as in any other friendship", including "small sums of money as gifts of friendship" but refuted claims that these were given in exchange for sex from his friend.

Moving quickly to pre-empt the *News Of the World*'s scoop, Brown admitted his sexuality and, like every other Labour Minister ever involved in a scandal, immediately received the full support and confidence of Tony Blair. John Prescott was set loose on the press and denounced them as playing "judge, jury and executioner" in the outing of gay MPs. Gordon Brown applauded Nick Brown's handling of the matter on the radio, and he also was said to receive the widespread support of his colleagues at Westminster; presumably including those MPs who took part in the homophobic campaign against McMaster.

*Tory Owl, http://the-tory-owl.livejournal.com/*

# Lord Irvine's Expensive Tastes

Alan Drew

How anyone could spend £300 on a roll of wallpaper, with a total bill of £59,000, is beyond imagination. But it didn't stop at wallpaper. Lord Irvine's official residence was restored to its original mid-19th century glory soon after his appointment. He spent £25,000 on a dining table, £16,000 on two beds and £140,000 on art. He spent £7,200 on lighting design, £56,000 for the fittings and £10,000 solely for "picture lighting". A £3,000 lavatory was installed, a further £8,000 on design and £23,000 on decorating. Just to recap – that's Twenty Three-Thousand Pounds on PAINT. Probably the strangest purchase, however, was £650 on "prototype curtain poles".

In total, he presented the tax payer with a £650,000 bill. Of course, Lord Irvine justified the expenditure as essential because the apartments were part of national heritage and used for public functions.

It later emerged that Lord Irvine had made the contractors sign the Official Secrets Act and insisted upon commercial confidentiality clauses. This proved a further thorn in the side at a time when the Government were drawing up the Freedom of Information Act. The Lord Chancellor was also called upon to apologise to the DIY industry, after justifying the expensive wallpaper as quality merchandise, unlike their products which might fall apart after a year or so.

Now, the notorious wallpaper is to dignify the Westminster equivalent of a works canteen.

But this isn't the true scandal of the Lord Irvine affair.

In October 1997, he delivered a cringe-worthy speech at the Reform Club, in which he boasted of his close relationship with Blair and his position at the "cusp of government". He even compared himself to Henry VIII's Lord Chancellor, Cardinal Wolsey. Lord Irvine was safe because he was subject to a journalistic convention that precluded any media coverage. However, he, in his usual arrogant manner, decided he didn't need the protection – he handed a copy of the speech to a *Times* reporter, inviting her to quote freely from it.

In March 1998, he made a televised appearance before a Commons committee. When defending the cost of his renovation, Lord Irvine proclaimed "We are talking about quality materials, which are capable of lasting for 60 or 70 years. We are not talking about something down in a DIY store which may collapse after a year or two". He just couldn't keep his head down, could he?

In the run-up to the 2001 general election, Lord Irvine wrote personally to Labour-supporting lawyers, inviting them to a £200 fund-raising dinner. Not only did he solicit donations from barristers whose career prospects depended on his patronage, he did not even understand that there was a problem. He told Parliament "I do not believe that I have done anything wrong. Nor do I believe I have broken any current rules."

And, finally, on a number of occasions he has attempted to sit as a Law Lord whilst being the Lord Chancellor, making him responsible for legislating and executing the law. He only withdrew when he was threatened with legal action.

The true scandal is, "the boy", as Blair was dismissively referred to by Irvine, didn't do anything about it. Perhaps Blair subconsciously felt that he owed Irvine a debt – he met his wife Cherie while they both were working in Irvine's chambers and he had borrowed money from Irvine to buy 'Myrobella', the Blair's Sedgefield home. But debt or no debt, Blair dropped Irvine from the Government in 2003 and replaced him with his other best mate, Lord Falconer.

# Ron's Moment of Madness

Steve Nowottny

The problem with BBC sleaze coverage is that, when it comes to sex scandals, Auntie really doesn't know where to look. It can't avoid them exactly, not when heads roll at a Cabinet level. But it prefers to blame others, and hide behind a montage of tabloid press headlines. Squirming with embarrassment, its journalists prefer to report politicians' denials of allegations they never made.

Never more was this true than in the strange case of Ron Davies, Secretary of State for Wales who in October 1998 became the first minister to resign from the New Labour Cabinet. According to the BBC account, "Mr Davies told police he was robbed at knifepoint after meeting a stranger as he strolled on Clapham Common and accepting a dinner invitation on Monday night."

Whenever a minister is under threat nowadays, of course, the press is quick to hark back to the halycon days of ministerial responsibility, and back in 1998 fresh-faced New Labour held themselves to a higher standard. But even then, being robbed at knifepoint wasn't considered a resigning offence.

The truth, unfortunately,

WELL, I WAS JUST OUT LOOKING FOR CABINET MINISTERS, WHEN SUDDENLY...

CLAPHAM COMMON

was somewhat more tawdry. Davies, who in 1999 admitted he had been bisexual at the time, was suspected of cruising Clapham Common for gay sex.

The full story, perhaps, will never be known, but in seeking to draw a line under the incident by describing it as "a moment of madness", he was probably writing his epitaph. And while politicians of every stripe declared that a man's private life is, well, private, in reality, caught in the media's spotlight, he was forced to bow to the inevitable. Before Oaten, there was Davies.

After quitting the Cabinet, Davies left his wife, resigned as an MP and reinvented himself as a member of the Welsh Assembly. But he wasn't, so to speak, out of the woods, yet.

In March 2003 he was caught again (see page 84), in a common cruising spot known, to the delight of tabloid sub-editors everywhere, as Tog Hill. This time there were photos, and witnesses. Davies's excuse? He was "looking for badgers". A euphemism not even the BBC would buy.

# Pinochet Set Free by Jack Straw

Christopher Doidge

Jack Straw, as Home Secretary, put political expediency above common sense when General Augusto Pinochet was arrested in the UK in 1998. The case bounced around various courts for 16 months, based on a Spanish judge's international arrest warrant, which accused Pinochet of 94 counts of torture.

Initially, Straw entertained those who enjoyed the sight of a 90-year-old imprisoned at Her Majesty's pleasure. But nearly a year and a half after Pinochet came to the UK for medical treatment, Straw performed a spectacular U-turn and eventually let the former dictator walk free, supposedly on grounds of ill-health. External medical experts and lawyers disagreed with Straw's judgment, and accused him of wanting to get rid of his biggest headache, which was creating waves across much of the world. His judgment also contradicted the ruling made by the House of Lords, which had said he was fit for trial.

Straw's position was made complicated by the apparent legal loophole which gave the Home Secretary the role of judge and jury in the case of whether Pinochet should be sent for trial. And while Straw argued the decision would be a wholly legal one, many believed politics was at play. Straw also had to deny allegations that his student past meant he was biased against the general's regime, whom he had protested against in the 1960s. Straw was believed to be a vocal supporter of Salvador Allende, the former Chilean President who died in Pinochet's bloody coup of 1973.

Oddly, Chile itself was against the extradition of Pinochet, and on his return he wasn't sent for immediate trial. Proceedings slowly continued until May 2004 when an interview given by Pinochet to a Miami television station indicated he was easily able to stand trial.

Jack Straw, on the other hand, was later found guilty of numerous poor appearances on television and eventually imprisoned with the role of Leader of the Commons, where he would serve out his time in the political wilderness.

*http://blogs.warwick.ac.uk/cdoidge*

# New Labour Sleaze in . . .

# 1999

## Tony's Sleazeometer, 1999
4 sleazy episodes: Straighter Guy, But Still a Quite Wobbly

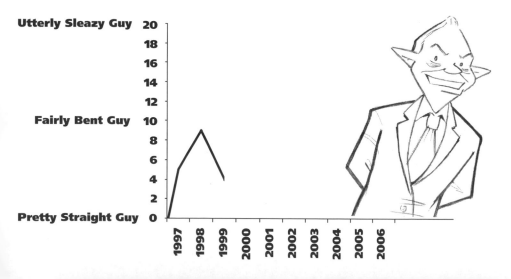

Utterly Sleazy Guy — 20, 18, 16, 14, 12

Fairly Bent Guy — 10, 8, 6, 4, 2

Pretty Straight Guy — 0

1997 1998 1999 2000 2001 2002 2003 2004 2005 2006

# Joan Aitken

Michael Hoskin

The selection of Labour candidates for the first elections to the Scottish Parliament in 1999 raised a number of eyebrows. Many highly regarded Labour politicians were told that they were not acceptable, but the convener of the selection panel, Rosemary McKenna, managed to find space for her own daughter.

One of the successful candidates on Ms McKenna's panel was Joan Aitken, a 46-year-old solicitor, who was selected to fight the seat of Inverness East, Nairn & Lochaber. At the Westminster Parliament, this seat had been gained by Labour from the Liberals in 1997, and Labour was confident of holding it in the Scottish Parliament elections. But in the event Ms Aitken was not elected, being defeated by the SNP in what was the only seat that the nationalists managed to win that they did not already hold in Westminster.

Fortunately for the Labour Party, its dominance in the Scottish establishment ensured that a public role could be found for Ms Aitken within months of her election defeat. In November 1999, she was appointed as the chair of the Scottish Prisons Complaints Commission, where she stayed for over three years before becoming the Traffic Commissioner for Scotland. On this occasion, questions were asked in the Scottish Parliament about the role played by the Scottish Executive in her appointment – but in typical Labour style north of the border, it was glossed over as it was evident that being rejected by the voters need not prevent a Labour Party hack from wielding considerable influence at public expense.

*Mikey's Tent of Reality, http://michaelhoskin.blogspot.com/*

# Junket Jack

Iain Dale

We all know that Jack Cunningham likes the good things in life. And why not? After 18 years out of power who could blame him if he wanted to enjoy the trappings of power? But sometimes you can just take things to excess and that's just what Dr Jack appeared to do, when in January 1999 the *Sunday Times* published allegations of high living at the taxpayers' expense. His civil servants had leaked lurid details of his use of top-class hotels, restaurants and flights. The newspaper reported that he flew to the US on Concorde, stayed at the five-star Conrad Hotel in Brussels the previous year and ate at a two-star Michelin restaurant – all at taxpayers' expense. The newspaper report followed previous claims that Dr Cunningham decided to take private jets instead of scheduled flights to European Union meetings when he was Agriculture Minister. Sadly for Dr C, his luck soon ran out and he was dispatched to the back benches a few months later.

*Iain Dale's Diary, www.iaindale.blogspot.com*

# It's a Hard Life

Iain Dale

Y ou know what it's like. You've been out of power for a generation. You just want a slice of the action. And in their first two years boy did Labour ministers get a piece of the travel action. In 1999 the *Guardian*'s David Hencke reported that ministers had spent more than £11 million on ministerial travel in their first two years in power. Take John Prescott – and we do wish someone would. Mr Prescott's first trip abroad, to India, cost a whopping £99,000. We know he's a porker, but surely even he only took up one first-class seat! He followed this trip by a little scuba diving jaunt to the Maldives costing a mere £6,925. The Deputy Prime Minister followed this up with a £12,000 junket to Rio de Janeiro, Brasilia, Sao Paolo, Miami and Washington. Hencke reported that the trip "included meetings with the directors of the Cunard cruise ship company, whom he once served as a bar steward". His cheapest trip was £940 for an overnight stay in Warsaw to discuss climate change. And I always thought Polish hotels were cheap.

The cost to the taxpayer of Robin Cook's dash back to London from accompanying the Queen on a royal visit to India in 1997 to meet his then mistress, Gaynor, was £3,849. At the time, Mr Cook said he had to return to take care of urgent constituency business. Monkey business, more like.

He surpassed himself a few months later by travelling with 14 officials to the Far East in September 1997 at a cost of £169,186.

The then Culture Secretary Chris Smith also liked the high life. He seemed addicted to visiting Cannes, spending £7,000 on three separate jaunts. He also spent more than £20,000 promoting tourism and the arts in Japan and the USA.

It's a hard life being a Labour Cabinet Minister.

*Iain Dale's Diary, www.iaindale.blogspot.com*

# New Labour Sleaze in . . .

# 2000

## Tony's Sleazeometer 2000

10 sleazy episodes: Fairly Bent Guy

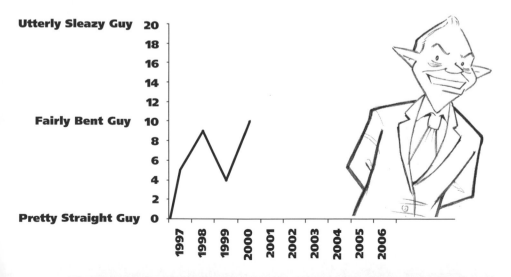

# Gordon Brown's Maxwell 'Connection'

Tim Rowell

In 1992, Gordon Brown displayed his *prudent* credentials when he bought himself a pied-à-terre in Westminster from the administrators of AGB Research, a polling firm that had recently been forced into liquidation. He bought the flat on the corner of Marsham Street and Great Smith Street in Westminster for the apparently cheap price of £130,000.

The deal began to look suspect, however, when the *Sunday Times* reported in January 2000 that AGB Research had been part of Robert Maxwell's business empire and had entered administration following Captain Bob's death a few months earlier in November 1991. Furthermore, on the board of directors of AGB Research had been a certain Geoffrey Robinson – the Labour Paymaster General – who had not only funded Gordon Brown's office to the tune of £600,000 but had also provided the infamous home loan to Peter Mandelson.

Gordon Brown released a statement denying any "impropriety in the deal" and stating that there had been "no discussion or communication with Geoffrey Robinson MP over the flat's purchase or its financing".

The Conservative MP David Heathcoat-Amory, among others, called for an inquiry but none was forthcoming.

Gordon Brown sold the flat for £350,000 in early 2002. A prudent deal indeed.

# Disgracefully Good Business

Jenny Geddes

Even if you are a disgraced Labour hack there is enough forgiveness in the party for you to scratch some form of living... as long as the public is paying. In January 2000 Philip Chalmers, who earned £50,000-a-year as head of the Scottish Executive's strategic communications unit, was arrested by Strathclyde Police for being drunk at the wheel of his car in a red light district with a prostitute in the back seat. He did do the honourable thing and resign. You would think that thus chastised, he would start up something new in business away from the vagaries of public life. But no. Phil sees there's money to be made and his past employers see no problem in passing on business... after strict tendering rules are adhered to of course.

For it was in January 2004 that it became public that Schlumberger had hired the one-time adviser Philip Chalmers to run the Scottish Tourist Board's Visit Scotland website. The website is part of a Scottish Executive PFI contract, so just at enough arm's length to go: "Oh Phil Chalmers! I wondered what he was up to these days." But why keep a 'good' special advisor down. In August 2005 it was reported that Phil was heading a bid by French IT firm Atos Origin to secure some of the ID card contracts. We wonder how he will get on.

# Prescott's Union-Owned Flat

Jenny Geddes

Deputy Prime Minister John Prescott, the token-working class member of the Cabinet, maintained his trade union links by renting a flat from one of them at well below the market rate – but he chose not to declare this benefit in the Register of Members' Interests.

Prescott was a steward in the Merchant Navy and started his political career in the National Union of Seamen (NUS) in the late 1960s. After being elected to Parliament in 1970, the NUS sponsored him as an MP and provided him with a flat in Maritime House, a block in now fashionable Clapham Old Town. The flat was provided on a statutory 'secure controlled tenancy', ie the rent is kept below the market rate.

The NUS later merged to become the National Union of Rail, Maritime and Transport Workers (the RMT), but Prescott continued to enjoy the benefit of the flat – and the benefit of the below market rent: in 2000, Prescott was paying £220 per *month* for the flat – a figure which had not changed since 1992 – while it was estimated that a similar flat on the open market would have cost nearer £220 per *week*.

In 1997, Prescott moved out of the flat and into grace-and-favour government accommodation in Admiralty Arch. But he held onto the flat and allowed his son to live there, rent free. No one seems to have asked ordinary RMT members what they thought about paying their union dues to help subsidise accommodation for Prescott's children.

Under Parliament's rules, MPs have to declare benefits given at a cost below that available to the public. When Elizabeth Filkin, the Parliamentary Commissioner for Standards, examined Prescott's case in April 2000, she said that Prescott should have registered the benefit he derived from the flat, at least from 1997 when he moved out.

Although Filkin found Prescott to be in breach of Parliament's anti-sleaze rules, her report went to the Commons Standards and Privileges Committee, which had an in-built Labour majority. They overturned Filkin's conclusion, but instead 'invited' Mr

Prescott to add the flat to his entry in the Register. Despite this polite invitation, Prescott has still never declared the interest.

The final twist is that Prescott, as Secretary of State for the Environment, Transport and the Regions, passed a law (the Rent Acts (Maximum Fair Rent) Order 1999) which further limits rent increases for such properties, thereby keeping down the cost of providing his son with a free flat.

John Prescott resigned from the RMT in 2002 and gave up the flat a year later.

# Speaker Betting Furore

Ross Fitzgibbon

Insider dealing in business is a criminal offence, for obvious reasons. In sport a competitor who is found to have placed bets on an event they have taken part in is usually hit with a lifetime ban. In Parliament they take a rather more relaxed view of things, as the betting scam that surrounded the elevation of Michael Martin to the role of Speaker illustrates. The office of the Speaker of the House of Commons is arguably the most important non-governmental post in Parliament – with the possible exception of Peter Hain's sun-bed maintenance man – and has the responsibilities of moderating debates and upholding the rules of the House in an impartial manner. When Betty Boothroyd stood down from the post in 2000 a new Speaker had to be chosen. Traditionally, the post alternated between the parties as a means of maintaining the neutrality of the office. As Betty Boothroyd had been a Labour MP it was expected that either a Tory or a Lib Dem would succeed her. A number of candidates were mooted including Sir Menzies Campbell and Alan Beith from the Liberal Democrats and Sir George Young and Sir Alan Haselhurst of the Conservatives. However, buoyed by the large majority from 1997 election, Labour MPs made it clear that they would not observe such a convention. Thus the ballot commenced with a record number of candidates

Candidates were voted for two at a time in a lengthy and gruelling process designed to sort the wheat from the chaff – which it did, albeit by discarding the wheat and electing the chaff. Michael Martin got the job having emerged as the man the BBC were describing as the bookies' favourite despite being a rank outsider just a few weeks earlier. It soon became apparent why. The odds from William Hill had gone from 20-1 to 8-11 as a result of several large bets – a total of more than £50,000, being placed throughout central Scotland and London.

An investigation by the Parliamentary standards watchdog, Elizabeth Filkin, found Labour MP Frank Roy had made one of the bets, but the identity of the other lucky gamblers remains a mystery. Roy felt that, "if the bookies are daft enough to offer odds like that then they deserve to lose money". He kept his job as PPS to John Reid and is currently a government whip.

# Smearing the WI

Chris Doidge

They jeered, they shouted and they certainly made their point. If only he'd spoken about cross stitch, post offices and crab apple jelly instead of the National Health Service!

Addressing the WI in June 2000 probably still brings Blair out in a heavy sweat after their booing and jeering forced him off the stage early during an important speech at Wembley Arena.

Beginning your speech with the words "This is the most terrifying audience I have ever seen in my life" is hardly the best way to win over an audience. And the tone of the speech continued to misfire, as Blair's words were seen by the ladies as "patronising" and full of jargon.

Recently returned from paternity leave after the birth of Leo, he was interrupted a number of times by large sections of the audience, who objected to the overtly political nature of the speech. Blair was clearly playing to the television cameras and ignoring the delicate tastes of the audience in front of him.

Some of the ladies walked out, shouting on their way, and the cameras performed a 180-degree turn. The event was a PR disaster, probably the low-point of the Alastair Campbell years.

But the real sleaze came from Number 10's feeble attempts to turn the ladies into the enemy, spectacularly failing to kill off the conventional view that the speech was a complete disaster. Rumours spread that the Labour Party had mounted a fierce attack on the ladies, digging the databases for dirt on the WI to give to left-leaning newspapers. Campbell's old employers at the *Daily Mirror* said Blair had been "set up", although even the *Guardian* admitted Blair had "bombed".

And the lecture was spun by Alastair Campbell and Co as just the speech that the WI had asked for. In desperation they tried to assert that the WI had made the original invitation to Tony Blair, although the WI had said that it was all Downing Street's idea.

Campbell played down the incident saying the WI incident showed that "a small number of people can get a disproportionate amount of attention." But the spin boomeranged when the mainstream press suggested the WI were merely the chorus leaders for a growing band of dissatisfied British voters.

*http://blogs.warwick.ac.uk/cdoidge*

# The Millennium Dome

Martin Curtis

*"If we can't make this work, we're not much of a government"*
John Prescott, June 1997.

*"We will say to ourselves with pride: this is our Dome, Britain's Dome, and believe me, it will be the envy of the world"*
Tony Blair, April 1998

Books could be written about the spectacular and continuing failure of the Millennium Dome, but the association of Robert Bourne with the failed sell-off attempt is worthy of particular comment.

Seven months before the Dome was due to close the Government announced that the list of preferred bidders for ownership of the site after the closure had been whittled down to two bidders – Nomura, a Japanese company and Legacy, a company set up by Robert Bourne with the Dome in mind. Shortly after that Nomura was given preferred bidder status.

After a short time and not a small amount of confusion, Nomura withdrew as preferred bidders, claiming that it was not given access to the Dome's accounts. You would have thought the shareholders of the Dome would be in uproar, but, then again, Lord Falconer was the sole shareholder. In November 2000 Legacy was nominated as preferred bidder for the site. The links between Robert Bourne and the Labour Party apparently had nothing to do with this, even though Robert Bourne had donated £100,000 to the Labour Party, was a friend of then Culture Secretary Chris Smith and had donated £6,000 to Smith's constituency Labour Party. It was also pure coincidence that Peter Bourne's wife, the theatre impresario Sally Greene, had previously hosted an extravagant birthday bash for Peter Mandelson.

After less than three months Legacy lost its preferred bidder status, giving the then Liberal Democrat Dome Spokesman, Norman Baker, the perfect opportunity to use the classic line: "To lose one preferred bidder is unfortunate, to lose a second is perhaps careless."

The Millennium Dome continues as a legacy to the failure of New Labour. Visitor numbers during its year of opening were projected at 12m, but only reached 6.5m (a large proportion of whom either gained free entrance or paid a reduced entrance fee). The costs while it was open exceeded the budget by £299m. Since closing it has cost around £35,000 a month to maintain.

It would be wrong to finish without acknowledging Peter Mandelson and Lord Falconer for their vital role in the Dome project. May it be a legacy to their competence and foresight.

*Spin Blog, www.martincurtis.net/blog/blogger.html*

# Byers Cooks the Books

Guido Fawkes

Stephen Byers is more recently infamous for his role in looting Railtrack shareholders (contemptuously called "grannies") but his name had already become a children's playground rhyme as far back as April 2000. Still till this day children in the playgrounds of the Midlands tease each other with the taunt "Liar, liar, you are Stephen Byers".*

Stephen Byers was Trade Secretary, Rover was, as usual, in crisis and BMW had taken over the firm but the terms were now in dispute. Byers claimed BMW had failed to adequately warn the Government about the dire situation. Byers' department released a copy of a statement from BMW's chairman, except it was different to the actual statement released by BMW in Munich. The details are lost in the mists of disputed civil service notes.

Byers was ceaseless in his efforts with regard to Rover, ceaseless in the sense that he sought to avoid any blame for the problems and ceaseless in denying he knew any of the facts that BMW had given him about the £2 million-a-day losses the Longbridge plant was suffering. Byers denied three BMW claims; that he was told that the Longbridge investment would be cancelled if a £152 million grant was blocked; that BMW had called him to warn him about the situation at Longbridge; and that he had been told Rover was "five minutes" away from disaster. BMW was lying in all three instances he intimated.

BMW was not happy with "the ultimate lying machine". The German car giant pulled out of its investment, unable to trust the word of a government minister who would think nothing of destroying their reputation to protect his. Rover limped on for a few years before closing down with the loss of thousands of jobs.

*www.order-order.com*

*This is a little lie, but as with all Stephen Byers stories, a lie is to be expected.

# New Labour Sleaze in . . .

# 2001

## Tony's Sleazeometer, 2001

11 sleazy episodes: Pretty Crooked Guy

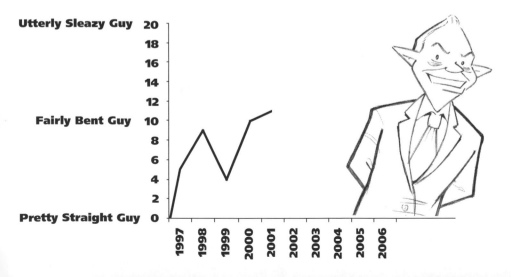

# As British as Apple Pie

Andrew Gardner

In 2001–02 the steel producer LNM Holdings

- Was owned by an Indian national, Lakshmi Mittal;
- Was registered in the Caribbean tax haven of the Netherlands Antilles;
- Employed over 100,000 people worldwide, but fewer than 100 in the UK;
- Successfully lobbied – through a US subsidiary – for tariffs on imported steel; tariffs which, according to Amicus, would be likely to cost 5,000 British jobs;
- Was the sister company of several that faced allegations of "dumping" (selling steel at unfairly low prices) by the US Department of Commerce;
- Was being sought by HM Customs & Excise for an unpaid VAT bill of £471,000;
- Was also being pursued by creditors – many of which were small British firms – over the largest corporate collapse in the history of the Irish Republic.

A company to treat with kid gloves, then?

Tony Blair didn't think so. In a letter dated 30th July 2001, he wrote in glowing terms to the Romanian premier, Adrian Nastase: "Dear Prime Minister, I am delighted by the news that you are to sign the contract for the privatisation of your biggest steel plant, Sidex, with the LNM Group. I am particularly pleased that it is a British company which is your partner."

*A British company…?*

Suitably reassured – the deal had been in some doubt – the Romanians signed a draft contract two days later. Details of Mr Blair's intervention – and of a contemporaneous donation of £125,000 by Mr Mittal – broke some six months on.

"The Prime Minister frequently writes to governments when British companies are competing for contracts abroad," huffed a Downing Street spokesman. "It is plainly in Britain's interests for him to do so. I do not know if he was aware of Mr Mittal's donation but it is irrelevant."

*British companies…?*

Even New Labour realised such a transparent fiction wasn't going to fly, and in subsequent statements LNM metamorphosed into "a British-based company"; though, save for Mr Mittal's ownership of a Hampstead mansion, it was hard to see in what way this was any more true. Pursuing the issue in and out of the Commons, opposition MPs met with the usual mix of evasion, stonewalling and, from Blair personally, haughty indignation. "It's not Watergate," he sneered across the despatch box. "It's Garbagegate."

And where there's muck there's brass; certainly for Mr Mittal whose empire has continued to grow. His donations to the Labour Party have risen too. They now (May 2006) stand at over £2 million.

# Two Jabs Prescott Strikes Back

Daniel Harvey

John Prescott's time as Deputy Prime Minister will be remembered for a number of incidents. The affairs, his wife's 300-yard trip by car to the Labour Party conference, having water poured over him at the Brits in a protest about the Liverpool dockers, and the day he hit an egg-throwing protester in 2001.

As usual, his timing was perfect. It was the day that Labour had launched their manifesto for the upcoming general election and Tony Blair found himself embarrassed when confronted by the partner of a cancer patient on a visit to a hospital, angry at the treatment he had received.

Prescott had been dispatched to Rhyl in North Wales, on his 'Battlebus', the so-called Prescott Express. On his way into a hall to address an election rally, Prescott was hit on the side of the head by an egg thrown by Craig Evans, a farm worker from Denbigh.

Fortunately for the media, and indeed Tony Blair, television cameras were there to capture the egg-throwing incident and also what followed next. Prescott was seen turning round and hitting Mr Evans in the face, with a well-aimed left jab. A scuffle ensued before the two men were separated by the police and Labour Party workers.

Prescott said: "I was attacked by an individual. In the melee that followed I clearly defended myself."

Both Mr Prescott and Mr Evans were questioned by the police, but no further action was taken. When questioned at a later press conference Tony Blair shrugged off the incident, saying "John is John". Very clearly.

# "A Muddle, Not a Fiddle"

Holyrood Watcher

L ooking back upon it now, nearly five years after the event, nobody really remembers why the Rt Hon Henry McLeish MSP, First Minister of Scotland, felt obliged to resign in November 2001. The affair became known as 'Officegate' and related to the fact that, while a Westminster MP between 1987 and 1999, Mr McLeish had failed to net off the rent he received for sub-letting part of his constituency office in Glenrothes before claiming reimbursement from the House of Commons. The total sum involved amounted to only £36,000 over more than ten years, so it was not as if McLeish would have been able to indulge a taste for Ferraris and dinners at the Ritz. And, in any case, he was more than willing to accept the Commons Fees Office's assessment of any outstanding payments due, once the mistake had been uncovered.

No, there were three reasons that McLeish had to go. First, the Scottish media had worked themselves into a feeding frenzy over the affair, spurred on by the Scottish Tories (particularly Tory leader David McLetchie who subsequently had to fall on his own sword over the equally trivial issue of taxi fares) demanding that McLeish produce ever more irrelevant details of his expenses claims. Second, McLeish had not distinguished himself in office, having developed a reputation for the occasional gaffe. But third, and perhaps most importantly, McLeish as a Fife MP and MSP was not part of the West of Scotland Labour mafia and therefore did not command the support of his backbenches and indeed of some of his Ministers.

Looked at with hindsight, the affair is not one from which the Scottish political system and the participants in it emerge with any credit. A decent if uninspiring First Minister was forced out of office for carelessness. McLeish said at the time that it was "a muddle, not a fiddle"; in truth, it was more of a guddle.

*Holyrood Watcher, www.holyroodchronicles.blogspot.com*

# Filkin Filleted

Chris Whiteside

Elizabeth Filkin faced systematic obstruction when investigating allegations against MPs as Parliamentary Commissioner for Standards. She became first a symbol, then a victim, of a toxic political culture in which maligning the integrity of your opponents has become a routine part of campaigning. Her treatment amounts to constructive dismissal and is a Labour Sleaze story for three reasons:

1  Obstruction of her investigations of Labour ministers, notably Keith Vaz, was inexcusable
2  Those who made Elizabeth Filkin's position so untenable that she did not seek reappointment, including the Leader of the House, Robin Cook, the Speaker of the Commons, Michael Martin, who banned her from publishing a letter listing how her investigations had been obstructed, and former speaker Betty Boothroyd, were all elected as Labour MPs
3  Almost worse than her removal was the manner of it. Instead of an open refusal to reappoint Elizabeth Filkin, her position was made impossible while Labour ministers claimed that the decision not to apply for reappointment had been hers. Where her predecessor, Gordon Downey, had been encouraged to accept a second term (he declined on grounds of age), Mrs Filkin was told she would have to reapply for her job in an open competition, although neither of the criteria which would have made this necessary applied. Speaker Martin's gagging order shortly afterwards was the last straw.

Mrs Filkin was to say after leaving that a "whispering campaign" started against her within weeks of her appointment, even before she published her first report.

"Some of the briefing was so ridiculous that it was funny before" she said. "People were saying I belonged to strange political organisations. It was bizarre."

Some resentment against Filkin arose because increasing numbers of complaints were submitted to her, and she appears to have been more thorough than her predecessor in investigating them all. Certain politicians of all parties resented being investigated as a result of allegations which they believed to be unfair. Tam Dalyell, one of the few who were entirely open in their opposition to Mrs Filkin's reappointment, accused her of investigating MPs on "frivolous, trivial and false grounds".

However, the real blame for this lies with the rival MPs who made the false allegations in the first place. Other MPs across the political spectrum from Tony Benn to Peter Bottomley thought her work was "exemplary". Bottomley was convinced she was forced out for being too effective.

*http://chris4copeland.blogspot.com/*

# Mandelson and the Hindujas

Martin Curtis

In early 1997 the Hinduja brothers expressed an interest in contributing to the Faith Zone at the Millennium Dome. At about the same time one of the brothers, Gopichand Hinduja, re-applied for a British passport (he had previously been turned down in 1990). The application was approved some eight months later.

Srichand Hinduja then applied in February 1998. In the same month the Hinduja Foundation made an offer to underwrite part of the Millennium Dome to the tune of £1 million. His passport application was refused. But the application was resubmitted in October 1998 and approved five months later. The Hindujas subsequently did sponsor the Faith Zone to the tune of £1m.

In 2001 some searching questions were asked about the events surrounding the Dome sponsorship, and the approved passport application was identified. Peter Mandelson had been responsible for the Dome as a Minister without Portfolio at the time the Hindujas' passports were approved, but by the time questions began to be asked he had resigned once and was beginning his second life in the Cabinet, this time as Secretary of State for Northern Ireland.

Peter Mandelson, of course, denied any wrong-doing and specifically denied playing a role in accelerating the application process. However, Home Office Minister Mike O'Brien recalled a telephone conversation with him in which the Hinduja passport applications were discussed. In a rare fit of genius, Peter Mandelson later remembered but continued to deny doing anything improper. As a result of the revelation about the telephone call Peter Mandelson was forced to resign for the second time. The irony of this is that the resignation was not forced because of proof of impropriety, nor from being exposed by the media, but because Alastair Campbell was made to look a bit silly when the news relating to the Mike O'Brien conversation became known.

As has often been the case with enquiries since 1997, Peter Mandelson was cleared of impropriety by Sir Peter Hammond QC. Alastair Campbell later claimed that

Mandelson's forgetfulness was due to the pressures of his role as Northern Ireland Minister.

Despite Peter Mandelson's propensity to fail, Tony Blair saw fit to appoint him as Britain's European Commissioner a short time later. Mike O'Brien's honesty in genuinely recalling a conversation that others denied is, of course, not the only reason he remains as a junior minister.

*Spin Blog, www.martincurtis.net/blog/blogger.html*

# Keith Vaz's Standards

James Fletcher

Nigel Keith Anthony Standish Vaz (Keith to his friends) has been the Labour MP for Leicester East since 1987 and found his way into hot water on two occasions. In February 2000, he declared £15,000 in the Register of Member's Interests for three £5,000 donations from Mrs Lakshmi Mittal, Charles Riachny – a Lebanese businessman – and a third unnamed donor. The only problem was that Piara Singh Clair, his local treasurer, had no record of the deposit.

Standards Commissioner Elizabeth Filkin investigated 18 allegations and cleared him on all but one charge: that of being in breach of the MPs' code of conduct for his failure to disclose small donations from Sarosh Zaiwalla, a lawyer whom he recommended for an honour. She also underlined his obstruction and unwillingness to co-operate. The Prime Minister and Foreign Secretary, Robin Cook, stood by the beleaguered Minister for Europe. At Prime Minister's Questions, Conservative leader William Hague suggested Mr Blair "could keep his government's integrity or his Minister". Mr Blair kept his Minister.

In March 2001, he was implicated in the Hinduja passport scandal where both Vaz and the newly rehabilitated Peter Mandelson were accused of helping Srichand Hinduja (who donated £1m to the Millennium Dome's Faith Zone) procure a British passport.

Elizabeth Filkin investigated 11 allegations, upholding three of them. She found that Vaz made a gross attack on the "integrity and reputation" of a member of the public assisting a parliamentary inquiry and may have wasted police time.

In addition, she found him guilty of "providing misleading information" about his wife's financial relationship with the Hinduja brothers, and that he "failed in his duty of accountability by refusing to submit himself to the scrutiny appropriate to his office as a Member".

Vaz was variously censured for intimidating a witness, misleading police, obstructing a parliamentary enquiry; and his pompous demeanour turned much of the media against him. At one stage he modestly described himself as "probably the most influential Asian in Britain". The *Sun*, while backing Labour at the 2001 election, virulently sought the removal of Mr Vaz. After the 2001 election, Vaz resigned as a Minister, citing ill health.

In 2002, as a result of the second inquiry, he was suspended from the Commons for one month and lost £4,318 in pay.

He remains an MP and is currently campaigning for the banning of a video game called *Bully*.

# Lord Drayson: Integrity, Integrity . . . er . . . Integrity

Guido Fawkes

You are a businessmen, you give a £50,000 donation to the Labour Party, so you get to have a business breakfast with the Prime Minister; you give a second donation of £50,000 to the Labour Party while the Government is weighing up who should be awarded a £32 million contract you are bidding on. Surprise, you get awarded the contract, you make £20 million profit on it. What value for money for the taxpayer, what a return on investment!

As fantastic as it seems, Paul Drayson gave the second donation of £50,000 to the Labour Party while the Government in 2001 was weighing up who should be awarded a £32 million contract to supply vaccines in case of a biological attack by terrorists. His company Powderject was bidding on the contract. Fortunately for him it did not go to tender. Kippers might not have been on the breakfast menu, but it was fishy enough for Powderject to get awarded the contract, making a quick £20 million profit on it. "New Labour, New War Profiteering" was the slogan.

Loaded now, Paul Drayson gave another £500,000 donation to New Labour, and was made a life peer by Mr Blair a mere six weeks later. The amazing life and times of Paul Drayson and Tony Blair has intrigued many people. Voters might want to find out what that breakfast meeting was about. That is after all what the Freedom of Information Act is all about. Was something fishy on the menu? We the people like to see what our rulers are up to, what deals they make. After all it's our democracy. The Parliamentary Ombudswoman agrees: "I consider that very little harm would be caused by the release of the comments attributed to [Lord Drayson] and that any potential harm is outweighed by the public interest in making that information available."

The government claimed to have shredded documents that could have revealed why the now Lord Drayson received the invitation from Downing Street. The Cabinet Office said: "Any other relevant documents had been routinely weeded and destroyed in accordance with normal records management and destruction policy". That is New Labour integrity.

The ennobled Lord Drayson was appointed as a Defence Procurement minister in 2005. The appointment was defended by Tessa Jowell, the Culture Secretary, who said Lord Drayson was a distinguished industrialist (translated, "big donor"). When Drayson sold Powderject, he did so via an offshore trust to avoid any tax being paid on the capital gains, saving millions. It is not known who advised him on the legality of that transaction. It would have to be an experienced international tax lawyer.

*www.order-order.com*

# Minto Street Affair

Phil Taylor

Our Scottish masters, the Scottish political types who wield undue power in Westminster, are not all-powerful. Nigel Griffiths, Labour MP for Edinburgh South, is one of the more mediocre and inept of them. He has spent most of the period since 1997 as a Parliamentary Under Secretary of State at the Department of Trade and Industry. An acknowledged Brownite, he was sacked from government in one of the early Blair-Brown power struggles in July 1998 only to be re-instated in June 2001. Another reminder, if one is needed, that this government has been wasting energy on fighting itself from the start. Besides his lacklustre ministerial career Nigel Griffiths's main claim to fame is the Minto Street Affair. Soon after his re-appointment in October 2001 it emerged that Griffiths's Minto Street offices had been used for campaigning purposes in contravention of House of Commons rules relating to expenses. At the time Griffiths got away with apologising to the Fees Office for using his constituency office during the election without their permission. Griffiths had been paying rent on these offices and reclaiming it from the Fees Office. In December 2001 the story re-ignited when Griffiths had to admit that he had owned the Minto Street premises and had not registered this fact in the Register of Members' Interests. He apologised at the time to Elizabeth Filkin, the embattled Parliamentary Commissioner for Standards. In February 2002 Griffiths was told by the Labour-dominated Commons Standards and Privileges Committee that he was wrong not to inform the Commons authorities that he owned the property which he was using at taxpayers' expense as a constituency office. Claims he submitted for office costs were "technically defective". But, predictably, the Labour dominated committee decided not to penalise Griffiths.

Note that Griffiths' ministerial progress was halted by the Blair-Brown feud but being sloppy with both the handling of money and the declaring of interests were no impediment. If Jack Straw's move to Leader of the House of Commons was seen as a demotion in the post-election reshuffle then Griffiths' move to be his deputy must be seen likewise. Nigel Griffiths continues to bump along the bottom of government.

# New Labour Sleaze in . . .

# 2002

## Tony's Sleazeometer, 2002
7 sleazy episodes: Not At All Straight Guy

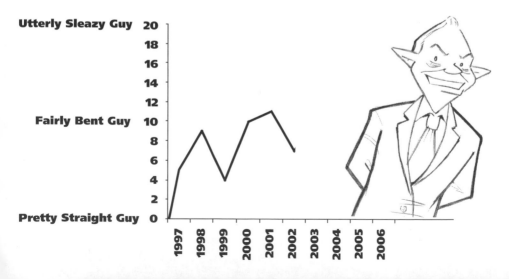

# Dirty Des and the 100,000 Big Ones

Andrew Gardner

"If someone is fit and proper to own one of the major newspaper groups in the country," Tony Blair told *Newsnight*'s Jeremy Paxman on 16th May 2002, "there's no reason why we shouldn't accept donations from them."

Shifting swiftly away from specifics, Blair proceeded to explain that it was really all the taxpayers' fault anyway. If only we weren't so mean as to object to state funding, there wouldn't be a problem, would there? He wouldn't have to grub around for cash the way... oh, the way Cherie and he had to grub around for a millionaire's villa each August. (The if-only-taxpayers-would-stump-up line of defence would be disinterred in the 2006 loans-for-peerages scandal.)

On this occasion, Blair had good reason to want to change the subject.

The "fit and proper" owner in question was none other than Richard Desmond, expletive-prone publisher of both the Express Group and an interesting range of other titles. One of these, *Asian Babes*, turned out not to be an academic study of childbirth on the subcontinent. Nor was a second, *Skinny & Wriggly*, a biography of Peter Mandelson. In common with *Mega Boobs*, *Horny Housewives*, *Big Ones* and 33 other top-shelf titles, they in fact constituted integral parts of Desmond's flourishing empire of erotica.

"I cannot understand why legal commercial operations, because some people don't find those activities morally acceptable, should be excluded from participating in the democratic political activities of their country," declared an unusually on-message Glenda Jackson.

Baroness Kennedy, Alice Mahon and even Tessa Jowell were rather less sanguine, but most of the sisters took Jackson's line. Some, indeed, when quizzed on the matter, seemed to be contracting lockjaw live on air.

But who exactly had decided Richard Desmond was a "fit and proper" person to own Express Newspapers in the first place?

None other than Stephen Byers, it emerged. Then Secretary of State at DTI, it was he who had waved through the takeover.

So the fact that Desmond had donated £100,000, or the newspaper supported Labour, or that the Express Group went on to appoint the Labour Party's former General Secretary, Margaret McDonagh, as the group's General Manager had nothing to do with anything, of course.

Coincidences all, insisted the spin doctors.

# Cheriegate

John Angliss

Traditionally, soap opera lifestyles have been the mainstay of models and fading pop stars. That the boyfriend of the "style guru" of the wife of Prime Minister Tony Blair could attract such media attention amply demonstrates that high-ranking politicians have just become another source of debased entertainment. "Cheriegate" was an excellent example. Working from within a rich patchwork of lies, both Cherie and Peter Foster, an Australian businessman from within her inner circle, tried to mislead a British media which already had evidence of the truth. Beginning with a fairly innocuous row over the price of some Bristol flats, this protracted scandal would lead to the Blairs having to reassess who their friends were.

On 1st December 2002, the *Mail on Sunday* alleged that "convicted fraudster" Peter Foster had used the Blair name on Cherie's behalf to gain a £20,000 discount on each of two luxury flats in Bristol, which Cherie wanted to buy for her Bristol University-bound son Euan. Downing Street sent out a series of red herrings before finally claiming that Cherie would have used her lawyer if she was to ever buy flats. Two days later, email correspondence was published in the *Daily Mail* which proved that the purchase had happened with Cherie's participation. Having purchased the flats through the Blairs' blind trust, Foster had in fact helped to secure a whopping £69,000 discount.

Peter Foster had been jailed four times for his trademark violations and breaching trading standards, often by promoting weight-loss pills with faked scientific backing. He was best known in Britain for having dated Page 3 stunner Samantha Fox, but was now facing the humiliation of deportation back to his native Australia. Cherie Blair stated she had only met him once "by chance" and Tony Blair told the House empathetically that "at no point did Mrs Blair interfere in the immigration case proceedings". On 11th December, Cherie suddenly appeared at a hastily arranged press conference at The Atrium restaurant near the House of Commons and proceeded to apologise to the nation, saying that she was "not superwoman" and denying that she had "taken up Mr. Foster's case". At one point she broke down, but quickly gathered her composure.

The following day the *Scotsman* alleged that she had personally given Mr Foster legal advice on his defence case. Both his lawyer and Downing Street denied this. The *Sun*'s transcript of Peter Foster's telephone calls showed that he not only had involved Cherie in his case, but he was also trying to sell the whole story to the media. Instead, he is now using it to complete his autobiography. Tony Blair was left aghast as those "parts of the media – and it is only parts – who take these grains of truth and on top of that [build] a whole mountain of distortion and half truth" appeared to have got it right.

# Pissed as Ken's Newts

Tim Rowell

In June 2002, the *Evening Standard* published a series of allegations about Ken Livingstone's behaviour at a 40th birthday party in London. Numerous eyewitness reports alleged that Ken had retired to a bedroom to recuperate at 11:30pm. On awaking at 1.30am Ken spotted his pregnant girlfriend (Emma Beal) smoking. A physical altercation ensued. Her friend, Robin Hedges, stepped in to protect her and a few minutes later he was found having fallen 15ft from the front steps of the house to the basement below. Ambulances and police were called to the incident. By the time they arrived, Mr Livingstone was not present.

The following day Robin Hedges released a statement through the Mayor's office. "The simple fact," said that statement, "is that I attended a 40th birthday party during which I had a fall and injured myself. It is false to suggest that anyone else was involved – it was an accident."

Two days later, Hedges retracted his earlier statement and alleged that he *had* been pressured into it. In an article in the *Evening Standard*, where he was employed as an Art Editor, he stated that Mr Livingstone had been involved and that he had been pressured into endorsing what he now maintains was an untrue statement by Ms Beal to protect Mr Livingstone.

In addition, he revealed that when he told Ms Beal he might press charges, Mr Hedges said Ms Beal told him that Mr Livingstone had said, "You may as well hold a gun to my head now."

During questioning at a special meeting called by the London Assembly Mr Livingstone said he would not be suing the *Evening Standard* for libel, or reporting it to the Press Complaints Commission because of "bad experiences in the past with such action".

# Alastair Campbell Meets His Match

Jonathan Calder

The Queen Mother died on 31st March 2002 aged 101. As she personified a century of British history, and in particular the victory over Nazi Germany, any media-conscious politician would want to be involved in the pageantry marking her passing.

Certainly, Tony Blair wanted to be involved. But he met his match in General Sir Michael Willcocks – the parliamentary official Black Rod – the man in charge.

On 13th April the *Spectator* published an article by Peter Oborne alleging Blair had tried to have arrangements for the lying in state altered to reflect his importance. The *Daily Mail* and *Evening Standard* took up the story, claiming Blair wanted to be at the north door of Westminster Hall to greet the Queen when she arrived.

Downing Street, though confirming there was discussion of Blair's role, complained to the Press Complaints Commission (PCC). The PCC deliberated and decided it could not establish the facts; Downing Street withdrew the complaint. Observers saw the affair as a no-score draw.

But Oborne had not finished. Another *Spectator* article claimed Downing Street had withdrawn because it feared Black Rod's evidence. Sir Michael had produced "a long, detailed and scrupulously documented memorandum that revealed the full details of how Downing Street tried to establish a bigger role for the prime minister".

No 10 continued to exude injured innocence. Between them Alastair Campbell, Peter Mandelson and Philip Gould ("Pass the Tippex, Mandy") produced a 29-page dossier rebutting Oborne's allegations.

The dossier was holed when readers noticed five pages in the name of a private secretary at the centre of an earlier row. She had asked civil servants to provide "killer facts" for Blair to use at Prime Minister's Questions.

And it sank when the *Mail on Sunday* published the gist of Black Rod's memo. Sir Michael told the PCC he had been subject to "sustained and constant pressure" from

No 10 over Blair's role at Westminster Hall. He had received more than a dozen phone calls, when the dossier admitted to only six.

Downing Street went quiet after that. Two senior Labour MPs – Tam Dalyell and Denzil Davies – called for Campbell to be sacked, and his reputation for competence was dented.

Sir Michael's name was missing when honours were awarded to those involved in the Queen Mother's funeral, but it was clear who had won.

*Liberal England, http://liberalengland.blogspot.com*

# Blackening Rose Addis

Julian Nicholson

"A dog… would have been treated better," was the line used by Iain Duncan Smith to describe the treatment of Rose Addis in January 2002. Addis, Ninety-Four, had been admitted to the Whittington Hospital on the 13th January following a fall at home, and the various claims made about her, and her treatment in the fortnight afterwards would be headline news for days.

Mrs Addis had suffered a cut to her head, and on arrival the wound was dressed, but not fully treated. Nothing scandalous there, you might think, some things just can't be treated fully immediately. The problem was, Mrs Addis' daughter, having been put off by the hospital, came to see her mother, and found her in the same bloodstained clothes she had been admitted in days before.

Mrs Addis' family went to the *Evening Standard*, which was then running a campaign about the poor state of London's hospitals, and the Standard broke the story; at the same time Mrs Addis' daughter had gone to see her local MP as she was unhappy at the response from the Whittington.

Of course, this doesn't make a massive scandal, and it was the response of the Government that triggered the escalation, as the Health Secretary Alan Milburn attacked the *Standard*, saying that the paper should "report facts, not fiction". This had two outcomes, first the *Evening Standard* counter-attacked, and the Addis family having failed to speak to the health secretary went, again, to Iain Duncan Smith, who then raised it at Prime Minister's Questions the next day.

In turn Tony Blair accused Iain Duncan Smith of exploiting the situation.

The most damaging aspect of the situation was to come out later, after rumours – spread by the Labour lie machine – that Mrs Addis had refused treatment because she did not wish to be treated by black or Asian nurses.

When the medical director of the Whittington, Professor James Malone-Lee was asked on *Newsnight* about the allegations that Rose Addis' refusal of help was due to racial motives he said that he could "imagine that people would deduce that". There was however, a massive fault in this attack, which was that Rose Addis was at that time being helped by two social carers from Hackney who were both from ethnic minorities.

The affair tailed out in the end as the Whittington's chief executive, Trevor Campbell-Davis, moved to apologise to the Addis family, and said that he "would not want the hospital ever to have given the impression that there was any racist overtone".

# Sorry, Sorry, Sorry, Sorry, Sorry . . .

Steve Garrett

J une 2002, time to apologise a lot. To paraphrase Oscar Wilde, to issue one apology is an honest and public recognition of a wrong done to others. To issue two seems a trifle excessive. Three is definitely gilding the lily of guilt. Issuing a full five seems to be taking things to hair-shirt-and-penance overkill.

But that's the amount of apologies heaped upon Paddington crash survivor Pam Warren by an apparently guilt-ridden New Labour Department of Transport. From the originator of the email right up to the former Secretary of State, Stephen Byers, a winning hand – a five card flush of apologies will beat almost anything else won't it?

A New Labour spin man had sent the email about Ms Warren and fellow members of the Paddington Survivors Group asking nasty little questions about their political affiliations. The email questioned their motives – hinting at a political edge to the Group's demands for railway safety reform. Dan Corry, one of Stephen Byers' extra-special advisors was the writer of the email – and when the document was made public, everyone who was anyone in the Department of Transport fell over themselves to register their abject hand-wringing from 'whiter than white' HQ.

It's the usual New Labour trick – if the information goes public and it contains particularly insensitive content then consult the Department Manual, Chapter 4, Appendix 2 entitled 'How to issue a grovelling apology for virtually anything'…

*www.wakinghereward.blogspot.com*

# "A Good Day to Bury Bad News"

Tim Roll-Pickering

"It's now a very good day to get out anything we want to bury. Councillors' expenses?" On September 11th Jo Moore, special advisor to Stephen Byers, Secretary of State for Transport, Local Government and the Regions, emailed out the above, suggesting that bad news could be released whilst the media's attention was focused on the tragedy in New York. It was to spark a row that only ended in the burying of her own career and eventually Byers' as well.

In October 2001, the email was leaked to the press, causing uproar. One relative of a victim of the September 11th attacks outrage over "basically burying bad news . . . under the bodies of six and a half thousand people."Such was the intensity of the row that Moore gave a public apology on camera stating, "I would like to sincerely apologise for the offence I have caused. It was wrong to send the e-mail and I accept responsibility for doing so".

But she smirked and the image went across newspaper front pages. The next day Tony Blair called the email "horrible, wrong and stupid," but stated that "sack[ing] someone and end[ing] their career [is] too heavy a penalty," declaring he considered the matter closed.

And there the affair would have rested but for a sequel the following February. On 13th February it was reported that Martin Sixsmith, the Department's Director of Communications, had sent an email stating: "Dear Jo, there is no way that I will allow this department to make any substantive announcements next Friday. Princess Margaret is being buried on that day. I will absolutely not allow anything else to be."

Although the actual text was misreported, the phrases stuck and reignited the whole affair. Reports that Moore was at war with civil servants left an image of a Department in chaos. That Friday Downing Street ordered the row settled. It was not just Princess Margaret who was buried that day but also Jo Moore's career.

The following year Channel 4 ran The 100 Worst Britons poll. Moore and Byers were ranked at number 59. Moore now works as a teacher in London.

Her departure may have removed her from storms at the Department of Transport, Local Government and the Regions but they would consume others until the Department was broken up at the end of May…

# "We're All Fucked.
# I'm Fucked.
# You're Fucked"

Tim Roll-Pickering

I t was not just Jo Moore's resignation that was announced on 15th February but also Martin Sixsmith's. It subsequently emerged that Sixsmith had not resigned after all. The row was to end in the resignation of Stephen Byers, whose name became synonymous with 'liars', as Secretary of State for Transport, Local Government and the Regions.

Sixsmith had spent most of his working life as a BBC foreign correspondent before becoming Director of Communications at the Department of Social Security in 1997. He subsequently worked in the private sector for Marconi before being appointed Director of Communications for the Department of Transport in December 2001. After the initial row about the Department's public image and the leaking of emails by civil servants, it was hoped he could restore order. However, just two months later the report of Sixsmith conflicting with Moore over releases of information reignited the whole affair.

On 15th February, Sixsmith returned from a hospital appointment to hear that both his and Moore's resignations had been announced by Byers. But Sixsmith had not resigned at all – he had been informed Moore was demanding his resignation as the price for her own departure and had merely agreed with Sir Richard Mottram, the permanent secretary that he would consider the matter after his hospital visit, with no action taken in the meantime. Mottram summed up the affair with: "We're all fucked. I'm fucked. You're fucked. The whole department's fucked. It's been the biggest cock-up ever and we're all completely fucked."

Sixsmith went public and denied his resignation, leading to a war over words as to who had said what. Byers came under immense pressure after his Commons statements were shown to be inaccurate. His Conservative shadow, Tim Collins, called it "the most clear example in human history of a man being caught out lying".

On 7th May, the Department issued a statement confirming Sixsmith had not resigned in February after all. Since Sixsmith felt it impossible to continue his job given the continuing public rows, he agreed to finish at the end of May. Two days later Byers was forced to give a statement to the House, but he refused to apologise. At the same time pressure was building on Byers after a critical report by the Labour-dominated Commons Transport Select Committee. Finally on 28th May he resigned.

Ironically, Sixsmith was still at the Department, working out his contract.

*http://timrollpickering.blogspot.com*

# New Labour Sleaze in . . .

# 2003

## Tony's Sleazeometer, 2003

11 sleazy episodes: A Pretty Crooked Guy . . . Again

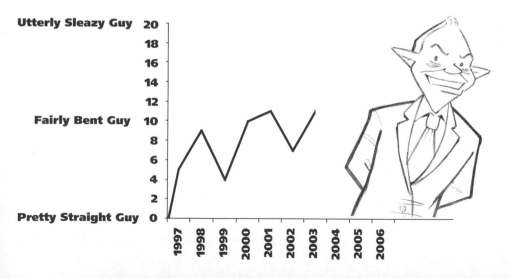

# The Ultimate Smear Test

Tim Ireland

When people want to know if that nice Mr Blair really condones torture, I begin by telling them the following true story. In August 2003 Craig Murray, the ambassador to Uzbekistan, was confronted with 18 charges, the most serious of which involved "hiring dolly birds for above the usual rate" for the visa department and granting UK visas in exchange for sex. Murray was forbidden from discussing (ie challenging) the charges under the Official Secrets Act, but that didn't stop a certain interested party from leaking those charges to the press... because shit sticks, even if the charges don't. (All but two of the most minor charges were dropped, and the Foreign Office eventually exonerated Murray of all 18 charges... but not before the smear campaign had taken a drastic toll on his health and reputation. Eventually, Murray was removed from his post for "operational" reasons.)

Compare this to the treatment of loyal soldiers David Blunkett and John Prescott... When it was proved that Blunkett was involved in an illicit affair that led to the fast-tracking of a visa for his former lover's nanny, Tony Blair described Mr Blunkett as a "decent and honourable man" who was leaving office "with no stain of impropriety against him whatsoever". When it came to light that Prescott had been dipping his cocktail sausage into staff members, Blair insisted that the ministerial code had not been broken and that it was "a personal matter".

What singled Murray out for such special treatment was his objection to the use of torture in Uzbekistan on our behalf. Murray argued that by accepting intelligence extracted under torture, we were enabling and justifying a murderous regime in exchange for intelligence that was fundamentally flawed in the first place and often spiced up after the fact. In his words, we were "selling our souls for dross".

One woman was raped (in the name of freedom, brothers) with a broken bottle in both the vagina and anus, and died after ten days of agony. An elderly man was suspended by wrist shackles from the ceiling while his children were "beaten to a pulp before his eyes". There were also numerous cases of 'suspected terrorists' being boiled alive.

In December 2005, when Jack Straw sought to "avoid getting drawn on detail" and "try to move the debate on", he made the following statement to the Select Committee on Foreign Affairs: "I have never had a piece of paper produced before me where on the rubric it says, 'We believe this has been obtained under torture'... "

Craig Murray reveals the truth behind this seemingly strong denial in a letter that the Foreign Office sought to remove from his memoirs: "I understand that the meeting decided to continue to obtain the Uzbek torture material. I understand that the principal argument deployed was that the intelligence material disguises the precise source, ie it does not ordinarily reveal the name of the individual who is tortured. Indeed this is true – the material is marked with a euphemism such as 'From detainee debriefing.' The argument runs that if the individual is not named, we cannot prove that he was tortured."

Blair's government did not launch any kind of investigation into Murray's allegations. Instead, it actually fought in the House of Lords for the right to act on intelligence obtained by torture abroad. And it fired Craig Murray for "operational" reasons.

This is why, every time I hear Blair assuring us that the perpetual war on terror is a global struggle to protect our sainted values, I don't have to imagine a boot stamping on a human face; instead, I am instead comforted by the very image of a broken bottle in my rectum. Forever.

I apologise if you now suffer from the same condition... but that's the reality of it.

*www.bloggerheads.com*

# 45 Minutes, Mr Bliar

Paul Linford

Controversy continues to rage about the 2003 Iraq War. Was it, as some still believe, a noble crusade to remove a brutal dictator who had terrorised his own people? Or was it simply the most infamous episode not just in the lifetime of the Blair government, but any British government since the Suez debacle of 1956?

Those of us who take the latter view do so largely on account of the so-called "dodgy dossier" published in September 2002, setting out the Government's case for war.

Actually, there were two dodgy dossiers. The phrase was also applied to a document published in February 2003, on the eve of the war, which turned out to have been lifted from a student's PHD thesis.

But the really dodgy dossier was the one which contained the really dodgy claim – that Saddam possessed strategic weapons of mass destruction capable of being fired at British targets within 45 minutes.

It achieved its desired result. "45 minutes from destruction" screamed the front page of the *Evening Standard*. A nation which had been in doubt about the war was hardened in its resolve. And it was all complete balls.

As the late Robin Cook said in his resignation speech, Iraq did not have any WMD in the commonly accepted sense of the words, and in publishing the 45-minute claim the Government had ignored the rather vital distinction between battlefield and strategic weapons.

A year and a half later, in October 2004, Foreign Secretary Jack Straw quietly withdrew the 45-minute claim – but by then hundreds of British lives had been lost.

Among them was Dr David Kelly, who realized the claim was wrong and attempted to correct it in conversations with journalists, setting off a chain of events that saw him become a pawn in a deadly battle of wills between Alastair Campbell and the BBC.

So was it a deliberate lie, or were Blair and Campbell just spectacularly misled? The Butler report, which found that caveats about potentially flawed intelligence had been purposely removed from the dossier, certainly suggested the former.

Either way, Blair will never be allowed to forget that he was responsible, unwittingly or not, for taking this country to war on a false prospectus.

Three years on, you could still hear the words "45 minutes Mr BLIAR" bellowed out at regular intervals by the anti-war protester Brian Haw in his long vigil outside the House of Commons.

*www.paullinford.blogspot.com*

# Donnygate

Ed Thomas

They accepted that life through the pits was gone for good, that the future lay in a blend of entrepreneurship and Government innovation. And what entrepreneurship, what innovation – only the biggest corruption scandal in local government of all time.

Not heard of it? Oh, well, that might have something to do with the media's attitude to New Labour scandals, and the fact that this was the era of 'classic' British films like *Brassed Off*, where the big enemy was the Thatcher years. This wave of nostalgia and emotion, combined with entrenched political interests at all levels, excused anything you care to mention.

It began, as much New Labour aspiration did, during the dark period surrounding the miners strike in 1981, and ended in 2003 with at least 31 convictions for offences ranging from (at the lowest end) expense fiddling, through planning corruption, contract fraud and misuse of public money.

When challenged by the Opposition concerning local government fraud, a New Labour spokesman sneeringly told the BBC: "This latest Tory cuttings job is more of the usual desperate and inaccurate rubbish. The Tories don't seem to have checked their facts properly."

New Labour MP Kevin Hughes responded to news of one of the arrests by saying "They'll be arresting people for taking a cup of coffee next".

According to former Labour Doncaster Councillor, playwright and whistle blower, Ron Rose, writing for Left-wing journal *Red Pepper*, "Donnygate involves the corruption of the whole democratic process".

He also notes "There has been no serious Labour Party investigation into the Doncaster scandals despite the enormous scale of the wrongdoing."

Of 31 people convicted, Rose reports that 25 were Labour councillors – and that others involved included prominent pillars of local Labour-supporting communities.

Had the 'democratic process' been truly operating, rather than being subverted by media spin-doctory and cronyism, this corruption would, and should, have cost Tony Blair dearly on a national as well as local level.

Doncaster Central has been represented in Parliament by former John Prescott "Office Director" Rosie Winterton MP since 1997. Doncaster North was represented by Kevin Hughes MP, who did not stand for re-election in 2005 and was replaced by Gordon Brown groupie Ed Miliband.

*Biased BBC, www.biased-bbc.blogspot.com*

# The Versatile Mr Bryant

Chris Palmer

December 2003, and *Daily Mail* readers that Christmas, along with visitors to Gaydar profile Alfa101, found themselves staring at the last turkey in the shop… well, almost. Chris Bryant, MP for Rhondda in Wales, was quite literally exposed by the Sunday newspapers at the time, with a photograph and stories leaving little to the imagination.

The former Church of England vicar, loyal lapdog of Tony Blair, described himself in his profile as "a fit bloke, bright, solvent, single, and very versatile" although, of course, the hard time he was hoping for compared to the hard time he actually received wasn't quite what he originally had in mind. Unfortunately for Mr Bryant, pulling out by taking his photograph and profile off the website was too late, and as a result, this later climaxed with calls for his resignation.

At the time, Bob McDonald, a Labour member of Rhondda Cynon Taff Council, said: "It is difficult to believe that a supposedly intelligent man would do this. I am amazed he would be so stupid." Another anonymous councillor told the papers, "The sort of behaviour he has engaged in here is not what you expect from an MP."

Throughout December, Chris Bryant faced growing pressure to stand down over his behaviour involving both the photographs and his virtual online cruise, which included sexually explicit emails to other potential cruisers, with remarks like "I'd love to meet for a good long fuck."

According to the *Daily Mail*, several MPs were using the pants photograph as screen-savers for their computers, and the *Guardian* commented "The political ramifications of using a website that treats gay sex like ordering a slice of pizza have yet to be seen" – though with the latest Mark Oaten scandal, we probably have a clearer idea.

At first Mr Bryant seemed relaxed with the situation which had thrust him into the limelight for all the wrong reasons, but the allegations had caused a certain amount of friction within his constituency. However, despite claiming he wouldn't be backing down in a hurry, Chris Bryant later issued an apology stating that his behaviour was completely unbecoming of an MP and public figure of his stature.

The former Caerphilly MP Ron Davies who was forced to resign from Westminster after his "moment of madness" on Clapham Common in 1998, due to allegations he groped a builder in the bushes at a lay-by came quickly riding to Chris Bryant's "rescue" when he claimed that he sympathised with his situation.

How touching.

*Political Crossroads, www.politicalcrossroads.blogspot.com*

# Tessa's Grants to Berlusconi's Film Company

Davide Simonetti

What connects Tessa Jowell with the corruption scandal engulfing her husband, David Mills, and Italy's ex-Prime Minister, Silvio Berlusconi other than mortgage shenanigans? David Mills is the lawyer behind Berlusconi's huge offshore business empire. Part of this empire is a major film company, Medusa, which received hundreds of thousands of pounds in grants from the British Government. Tessa Jowell, Minister for Culture, Media and Sport, is responsible for the UK Film Council which funded productions that were backed by Medusa. The UK Film Council, a Government-backed body which invests in British films using both lottery and taxpayer's money to the tune of £20 million a year, paid £110,000 to the British distributors of a film backed by Medusa called *Respiro*. It also invested £390,000 in a film called *Tickets*, a co-production with other British film companies. Both films flopped at the box office. Medusa also benefited from tax breaks given to Italian films made in Britain because of the 2003 UK-Italy co-distribution agreement signed by Tessa Jowell (presumably on this occasion she did know what she was signing). David Mills, who is already likely to be prosecuted for tax fraud and embezzlement regarding Mr Berlusconi's Fininvest and Mediaset companies (as well as perverting the cause of justice), has been shown by numerous documents to have played a role in Medusa. He is said to have "represented the company in negotiating contracts and commercial opportunities" since 1996 and before that was involved in the company's Dublin wing (now "de-registered") whose function was to set up tax breaks for Medusa. Not that we are suggesting there is anything wrong with this. After all, we know the government to be "whiter than white". They must be. The Prime Minister said so.

*Nether World, www.nether-world.blogspot.com*

# Cherie's Supermarket Sweep

Martin Curtis

Cherie Blair is of course extremely highly paid. We are also aware of the financial ambition that has led to her using her status as Prime Minister's wife to make a few quid in a totally unprecedented way.

She is not averse to the odd freebie either. On a visit to Australia in 2003 she was invited to visit the world-renowned Global International store in Melbourne. When offered the opportunity to "take a few gifts" Cherie embarked on a supermarket sweep that would have left Dale Winton whooping in admiration.

Trailed by two apparently excited children, Cherie duly helped herself to a total of 68 items, ranging from alarm clocks and pyjamas through to jeans and boxer shorts. In total she is thought to have helped herself to goods totalling £2,000.

Did she pay for them? Did she leave a token donation to charity? Did she declare them to Customs? This is Cherie we are talking about.

*Spin Blog, www.martincurtis.net/blog/blogger.html*

# The Death of Dr David Kelly 1

Tim Montgomerie

In 1996 Dr David Christopher Kelly was made a Commander of the Order of St Michael and St George in recognition of his service of the British state. Rolf Ekeus, a chief UN weapons inspector in Iraq, nominated Dr Kelly for the Nobel Peace Price. Dr Kelly survived working in some of the most dangerous parts of the world and with some of its most dangerous weapons. He did not survive a war of wills between Alastair Campbell's Downing Street spin operation and the BBC, however.

Dr Kelly's job description included a media liaison role and over years of overseeing weapons decommissioning he had built up many contacts. He used one of these contacts, Andrew Gilligan, to publicise his objections to the Government's infamous claim that Saddam Hussein could launch deadly battlefield weapons in 45 minutes. On the back of his meeting with Dr Kelly, Gilligan famously reported on the BBC *Today* programme on 29th May 2003 that Downing Street had "sexed up" the Iraq War intelligence dossier and that Alastair Campbell was the guilty man.

Alastair Campbell had been a bully throughout his time as Blair's spinmeister. Often referred to as the "real deputy Prime Minister" he enjoyed more influence on the Blair project than almost every cabinet minister. Campbell's fingerprints were all over Blairism's worst features. The briefing against opponents. The obsession with tomorrow's headlines. The distortion of statistics. The defence of the indefensible.

Campbell turned his whole PR operation against the BBC after Gilligan had made his incendiary allegations and, with a lot of help from Lord Hutton, he eventually succeeded in removing the BBC's top brass.

In the middle of this war David Kelly committed suicide although many conspiracy theorists, relying on expert testimonies, still believe that he did not end his own life. Dr Kelly was found dead near his Oxfordshire home – eight days after the Ministry of Defence had confirmed his identity to a hungry pack of journalists. The Whitehall machine exposed this private, retiring man to the hottest of media frenzies. The

Hutton Report was widely seen as a whitewash but even Lord Hutton concluded that the Ministry of Defence had failed to properly protect one of its key employees.

Alastair Campbell left Downing Street in August 2003 after the press and public had become sick of his media manipulation. His departure was spun as the end of the era of spin but the spinner returned to Blair's side for the 2005 general election. His return cost Labour donors £47,000.

*Editor, Conservative Home, www.conservativehome.com*

# The Death of Dr David Kelly 2

Richard Bailey

On 24 Sept 2002, the Government published an intelligence dossier containing the now legendary claim that the Iraqis could "deploy these weapons [of mass destruction] within 45 minutes of the decision to do so." On 29th May 2003, after the Iraq war, the BBC broadcast an unscripted live report by Andrew Gilligan on the Radio 4 *Today* programme, stating that "one of the senior officials in charge of drawing up the dossier says that the Government knew the 45 minute claim was wrong and a week before publication, Downing Street ordered it to be sexed up…" On 30 June 2003, after weeks of controversy, Dr David Kelly admitted to his boss that he had met Andrew Gilligan in an unauthorised meeting a week prior to the fateful BBC report.

To qualify for this book, an event must carry an element of sleaze rather than simply scandal. It is an unfathomable scandal that our Government might consider leading our country into war on a false or exaggerated prospect, but it is sleazy beyond belief for our Government machine, empowered by Tony Blair and his inner circle of advisors and loyal Ministers, to conspire to name and smear a top civil servant in a bid to save their own necks and hide the truth.

The pressure on the Government, on Blair, Campbell and Hoon was immense and increasing. On 8th July, the Ministry of Defence issued a press release stating that an individual official had come forward. Suddenly, an eminent government scientist had become a pawn in a vicious game between the Government and the BBC, with both attempting to force the other into revealing the name of the source and thus defend their own version of events. A supporting brief for MOD press officers contained the advice that if the right name is suggested by the media, they could confirm it. By 6pm the following day, Dr Kelly's name had become public.

In the final week of Dr Kelly's life, the Government's primary concern was the limitation of damage that might come from Dr Kelly's appearance before the FAC and Intelligence Select Committee and the complete demolition of Andrew Gilligan's reputation. As Campbell said in his diary entry for 4th July 2003 "GH (Geoff Hoon) wanted to throw the book at him [Kelly] but there was a case for getting a plea bargain. GH and I agreed that it would fuck Gilligan if that [Kelly] was his source."

Dr Kelly was cut loose by the MOD and left to cope with the pressure of media attention without any of the support afforded to Ministers and other public figures. It remains the Government's position that neither Geoff Hoon nor Tony Blair had any involvement in the media handling strategy that allowed Kelly's name to be confirmed to media should they suggest it first. It is stated that the Director of Communications at the MOD, Ms Pam Teare, devised the strategy herself without reference to or clearance by ministers.

I can only assure you that, as a former Whitehall press officer myself, there was no occasion on which any statement was given nor Question and Answer brief written without explicit and full clearance by the minister in whose name it would be released. I can also assure you that, as the press officer responsible for the Hutton Inquiry media arrangements, all the lines prepared for the event were cleared by senior officials at Number 10 Downing Street.

On 17th July 2003 Dr David Kelly walked from his house and committed suicide in the tranquil Oxfordshire countryside and plunged Tony Blair and his Government into the Hutton Inquiry and months of unremitting exposure. In his closing address, counsel for the Kelly family said that one of the aims of the Kelly family in the Inquiry was that the "duplicity of the Government in their handling of Dr Kelly should be exposed". The dishonourable, underhand and frankly incompetent way in which the MOD and Number 10 Downing Street handled Dr Kelly immediately prior to his death was revealed in all its glory, but no knock-out blow was ever landed in evidence to the Hutton Inquiry and the Government wriggled free, released by the Hutton report which was, ironically for New Labour, condemned as an Establishment whitewash.

*Richard Bailey was press officer to the Hutton Inquiry, www.baileyblogspot.blogspot.com*

# Badger Watching

Dave Robespierre

March 2003 – Ron Davies, the former Welsh Secretary, announced he would be leaving politics following newspaper claims that he took part in a gay sex act with a stranger in a public beauty spot at Tog Hill, just off the M4 north of Bath in Somerset. Davies claimed that initial denials that he had been in the area at all had been based on confusion: "I have actually been there when I have been watching badgers". For some reason, local papers were unable to publish the following "Country Diary" piece at the time of the Tog Hill incident. The short reflection on rural life and customs can now be reproduced in full for the first time.

*A Country Diary: Tog Hill, Somerset – by Cedric Gravel: To Tog Hill, the early spring morning sunlight dappling softly on the hidden telephoto lenses of that most shy of creatures, Sun photographers, as they conceal themselves in the lower bushes. As I sit and watch, I see one slowly emerging: small head, thick short neck, beady little eyes and long wedge-shaped body, yes, the European badger (meles meles) snuffles gently in the undergrowth unconcerned and unaware of the part-time plasterer from Bristol seeking a bit of rough trade in the mosses and undergrowth of this most attractive lay-by. Approaching now from the deeper undergrowth, small head, short thick neck and that familiar wedge-shaped body – it's our old friend, the Labour member for Caerphilly in the Welsh Assembly. The outcome of these couplings is predictable. Initial denial, claims of devastation and bruising and finally attaching all blame to the media. Other denizens of this wooded paradise will eulogise about the tragic end of a political career while the third wife will wonder what the hell she's let herself in for. At some point the swines from the local constabularly will be involved, names in paper, etc. Nature red in tooth and claw, the vicious cycle of life in the undergrowth . . . I remember when Bertie and myself did our trip to the Ardennes just before the War, we (that's enough this week, Cedric. – Editor).*

*The Happy Tumbril of Hubris, http://happytumbril.blogspot.com/*

# Not an Extremely Disturbed Person

Steve Garrett

In November 2003, Children's Minister Margaret Hodge was forced to eat upwards of twenty grands' worth of very public humble pie. Ten thousand went to a charity, the other half paid for Mr Demetrius Panton's court costs. The reason she swallowed this sticky, indigestible Hodge-podge of stodge was just payment for an utterly contemptible attempt to discredit an honest and honourable man. In a letter to BBC Chairman Gavyn Davies, she'd accused Mr Panton of being "an extremely disturbed person" Hodge has always been a bit intemperate, a bit gung-ho and a tad hasty with her use of language – but this episode really plumbed the depths. Mr Panton said, "I have experienced the personality politics of the gutter. I personally think that's not the kind of politics that we expect from the Minister of State for children." She sent the letter in an apparent attempt to stop the BBC from investigating Panton's claims of child abuse whilst he lived in Islington's care homes during the 1980s. Hodge was head of Islington Council at the time. The BBC programme would obviously have embarrassed Hodge, testy questions may have been asked about her involvement – especially as she had rather ironically and incomprehensibly been promoted to "Minister for Children" in Blair's whiter than white government. Typically, as with all New Labour ministers, Hodge refused to resign. Typically, as with all New Labour ministers, she received "full and unequivocal" backing from Tony Blair. Hodge's letter of apology was abject, grovelling and total in a desperate attempt to bring the matter to a close. Fortunately, Mr Panton is made of sterner stuff, he insisted on a charity donation, court costs and a very public apology to him. I wonder if Mr Panton has ever thought of running for Parliament?

*Footnote*: Tony Blair promoted Margaret Hodge in his May 2006 reshuffle.

*www.wakinghereward.blogspot.com*

# Fancy a Brazilian?

Chris Palmer

They say it's hot inside Brazil – and Clive Betts should know. In July 2003 he was suspended from the House of Commons for his part in a bogus immigration application by his Brazilian former male escort and lover – the same rent boy that he employed as his parliamentary assistant.

Caught out by the notorious *Sun* newspaper as a closet gay while holidaying in Venice with said rent boy, whom he loaned (yes, another one of these mystical Labour loans that never seem to need repaying) over £4,000 to apparently help with his "tuition fees" – the papers claimed that by applying for a security pass allowing the "former" escort to wander unescorted in Westminster, he was seriously undermining Parliament and breaching the MPs' Code of Conduct.

The Commons Standards and Privileges Committee agreed and found the MP for Sheffield Attercliffe had acted "extremely foolishly" in agreeing to photocopy a doctored document which his lover had hoped would help him extend his stay in the UK (which, guess what, it did) and attempting to gain a security pass easily misused in the wrong hands.

However, in Clive's own little world this was only "an error of judgement". How many times have we heard that from Labour before and since?

In the event Clive Betts apologised to Parliament, claiming that because he effectively owned up (notably after being caught) and asked the Complaints Committee to investigate his disgraceful conduct, that made it OK… Well that make's everything all right then – obviously.

*www.politicalcrossroads.blogspot.com*

# New Labour Sleaze in . . .

# 2004

## Tony's Sleazeometer 2004

11 sleazy episodes: Still A Pretty Crooked Guy

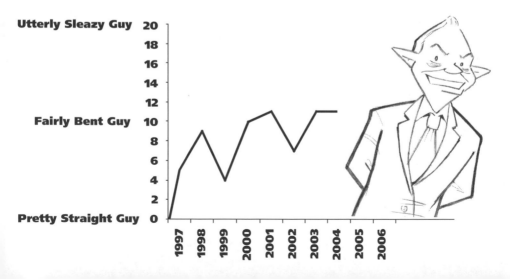

# The Resignation of Beverley Hughes

George Surgenor

The resignation of Beverley Hughes as Immigration Minister in April 2004 was shameful in many ways. Not only did she preside over a system that allowed thousands of bogus immigrants into Britain, she misled the public and then blamed her civil servants for her failings.

Hughes had been warned for more than a year that bogus immigrants from Eastern Europe were being waived through by the Home Office. Junior minister Bob Ainsworth had sent her a two-page memo warning that staff had been "demoralised" at the "weakening of the immigration control". She had acknowledged this, though in her reply seemed to be more concerned with the entitlements of offenders and refused to inform the Bulgarian authorities of suspected bogus applicants, because it "raised human rights issues".

Her failure to act on these warnings prompted two civil servants to go public with the scandal. James Cameron, the British consul in Romania, claimed that "suitcase loads" of false applications had been waived through by the Home Office, despite earlier warnings. Cameron was recalled from Bucharest and given a final warning on his conduct. Steve Moxon tried to inform Hughes of fast-tracking in Sheffield, but his e-mails were ignored and he was refused a meeting. After initially denying such a policy, Hughes was forced to admit she had authorised such a policy, and then blamed it on the "excessive zeal of officials". Hughes blamed a secretary for not passing on Moxon's email and refused to apologise to him. Moxon was fired for "embarrassing ministers".

Hughes then misled the public, by announcing on *Newsnight* that she had not been informed of such abuse even though she had sent two letters of reply to Ainsworth. She announced that she was "neither incompetent nor dishonest", despite the fact that there was firm evidence of one and considerable suspicion of the other. Hughes previously ignored warnings before the death of the Chinese cockle pickers on

Morecambe Bay. She also condemned a Channel Four television programme as "unspeakably sick", before admitting that she had in fact not seen it. In spite of this, Blunkett saluted her "integrity" and said she had been an "effective minister". Cameron and Moxon were punished for exposing the scandal, Blunkett and Hughes were recalled to the Government after causing it. After the scandal, Prime Minister Blair promised to take "a close interest" in immigration matters, which no doubt explains the current shambles.

# Vote Early, Vote Often

Michael Moncrieff

T he desperation of the Labour Party reached a new low when Election Commissioner Robert Mawrey QC upheld allegations made by opposition parties that six Labour councillors had engaged in electoral fraud during the 2004 Birmingham Council elections.

Opposition supporters lodged petitions amid concerns over vote rigging and intimidation during the election, all of which were hotly denied by the Labour councillors involved. However, three of those being investigated had been found by police handling unsealed postal ballots in a deserted city warehouse. This 'vote-rigging' factory, was more successful than the other infamous Birmingham factory at the time (the Rover plant which Labour shamelessly threw money at in 2005 to secure votes) as the judge ruled that at least 1,500 votes had been fraudulently cast in a massive, organised scam. Judge Mawrey also declared that the elections to the wards of Aston and Bordesley Green, where all six were elected, were null and void, and ordered new ones in which they were not allowed to stand.

Since then, one of the men stripped of his council seat, Muhammed Afzal, has been cleared of all charges. The ruling on the others remains, that they collected postal votes for the election through forgery and deception. Both before and after the scandal, enquiries had highlighted how open the postal ballot system was to abuse. At the 2005 general election, John Humphrys was denied the right to vote over a postal ballot mix-up. Since then, concerns have been raised in London, Stoke and again Birmingham about the possiblity of postal vote fraud. The government claims to have tightened up the system, but the stench of sleaze still hangs heavy over the Labour Party following their fraudulent behaviour in Birmingham's 2004 election.

Surely there is nothing so sleazy as having to rig an election to ensure victory?

# Paying for it

James Cleverly

She was one of the 101 female MPs who were swept into office on the crest of the 1997 New Labour wave. They were dubbed "Blair's Babes" and the implied criticism was that they were just window dressing, only there only to make the Labour Party look good. Indeed many of these female MPs were surprise additions to the Labour benches having stood in seats which no one at the time expected to turn from blue to red. Oona King was never someone who could be described as window dressing. With a first class degree in politics and years of experience in the European Parliament she was clearly one to watch. And watched she was. It seems that despite her intelligence, qualifications and experience at least one Labour MEP saw her basically as a "shag". She is, after all, very attractive. Sir Robert Walpole once said that "Every man has his price" and this particular MEP was keen to find out if Oona had one too. But how much to offer? Too little could result in a refusal, too much would get the desired result but would leave the nagging feeling that you could have got a better deal. Our randy Labour MEP came up with the ideal solution, offer a huge amount of someone else's money. The figure was £10,000 and the money was yours. Now as I have said (too often if my wife is to be believed), Oona King is an attractive woman, but £10,000 is a lot of money. A lot of your tax money. Oona told him to "go to hell". Supermodel Linda Evangelista once declared that she wouldn't "get out of bed for less than $10,000 a day". It seems that our Oona won't get into bed for £10,000. And who could blame her?

So what have we learned from this little episode? That there were some randy Labour politicians who thought nothing of propositioning their subordinates? That there were some people in the Labour Party who thought nothing of spending thousands of pounds of public money for their own gratification? Unfortunately yes to both, but at least those days are behind them. (Shurely shome mishtake – Ed)

*www.jamescleverly.blogspot.com*

# What They Did on Their Holidays
Holyrood Watcher

It is often said that Scotland is a village. It was no surprise, therefore, to learn that Scotland's First Minister, Jack McConnell, and his family were friends with Scotland's first lady of broadcasting, Kirsty Wark, and her family. But eyebrows were raised when it became known that the McConnells had spent the New Year holiday at the end of 2004 with the Warks in the latter's Majorcan villa. The bold Jack saw nothing wrong in such an arrangement; indeed he did not even feel obliged to record it in the Scottish Parliament's Register of Members' Interests.

It seems not to have occurred to either Jack or Kirsty that their shared holiday might compromise their respective positions in the political and broadcasting worlds. And, for reasons which mystified most observers, the parliamentary standards commissioner deemed that the First Minister did not need to have declared the holiday. Wark, on the other hand, was apparently put on probation by the BBC and she was allegedly dropped from presenting the Scottish coverage of election night.

There are two lasting memories of the affair. The first involves the unanswerable question of why on earth would an obviously bright and successful media star want to spend a holiday with a hack politician like McConnell? The second involves further confirmation of McConnell's execrable taste in clothes. After his earlier fashion faux pas in wearing a pinstripe kilt in New York and thus embarrassing the entire Scottish nation, on this occasion he allowed himself to be photographed wearing beige shorts, white socks and trainers. As the First Minister is not exactly blessed with the physique of a racing snake, it was something of a mercy that the pictures were confined to the Scottish press.

*www.holyroodchronicles.blogspot.com*

# Lord Fire Starter

Bel Andrew

L ord Watson of Invergowrie was the Labour MSP for Glasgow Cathcart until he was sent to prison in September 2005 for setting fire to a hotel. He had previously been a Labour MP from 1989 to 1997.

It all began in November 2004, at the Scottish Politician of the Year Awards. The function was held at the Prestonfield House Hotel in Edinburgh. There was a private VIP function following the awards, to which the noble lord was invited. Drinks flowed throughout the evening, and Lord Watson took full advantage of the free bar.

The party ended, and the guests departed, but Lord Watson was not yet ready to leave. He stayed behind, aggressively demanding more drink as the staff tried to clear up. He refused to accept that the bar was closed, and frustrated staff ended up giving him a bottle of wine to get him off their backs. Fed up with his boorish behaviour, the organiser of the event was eventually forced to remonstrate with him. Lord Watson was not happy. He waited until everyone had gone, and then crept into the reception room. Crouching in the still night, he fished out some matches from his sporran and set the curtains alight. The fire caused about £4,500 worth of damage. Unfortunately for him, his every move was captured on the hotel's CCTV. Imagine his shock when the Police came calling. At first, he denied any involvement, but later changed his mind. He pleaded guilt to wilful fire raising, and was jailed for 16 months.

*Bel is Thinking, www.declaim.blogspot.com*

# Cherie Blair and The Goldfish Bowl

Tim Rowell

In 2004, Cherie Blair and the popular social historian Cate Haste (author of *Nazi Women* and Melvyn Bragg's wife) wrote a book entitled *The Gold Fish Bowl: Married to the Prime Minister*. On the face of it, it was an interesting, if rather pedestrian study of the contrasting experiences of the spouses of British Prime Ministers – from Clarissa Eden through to Cherie Blair and including the only male to occupy the role, Denis Thatcher.

What followed, however, began to mire the book, its co-author and the co-author's spouse in controversy. Cherie Blair embarked upon a 'world tour' to promote the book from Hay-on-Wye to Washington DC, and from Auckland to Florida. Invariably billed as "An Afternoon with Cherie Booth", Cherie was earning somewhere in the region of £750 per minute to give a short speech and answer questions about her life in Number 10 and her experiences of being married to the Prime Minister. In total, Cherie is believed to have earned in excess of £500,000 from her speaking tours.

Norma Major may have penned a book exploring the history of Chequers but never embarked on such brazen exploitation of her position.

The Blairs are believed to have a mortgage debt of almost £4million on their properties in London, Bristol and Sedgefield. Cherie earned roughly £30,000 per talk – that's roughly two months' mortgage payments. A very nice little earner.

# The Lies Over Abu Ghraib

Robert Halfon

The Abu Ghraib debacle has been one of the most difficult episodes of the Iraq war – greatly undermining the justified humanitarian reasons for invading Iraq. It presented a propaganda gift to those opposed to the war. Yet instead of acknowledging the problem and the human tragedy that had occurred, Tony Blair pretended that his Government knew nothing about it.

On 12th May 2004, Tony Blair denied in the House of Commons that he or any other Minister had been informed about the allegations of the abuse of prisoners in Abu Ghraib. Yet this was far from the truth. It subsequently emerged that the then Foreign Minister Bill Rammell had been informed almost two months earlier.

On 18th March 2004 Mr Rammell had been given information about the alleged abuse by the President of the International Committee of the Red Cross (ICRC). On 19th March, the Foreign Office was given a report about the abuses by the ICRC.

It beggars belief that Mr Blair, or the Foreign Secretary Jack Straw, was not told about about the ICRC Report, unless Mr Rammell failed to tell the Foreign Secretary. In fact, on 11th May Jack Straw said that he should have been given a copy of the report.

Even giving Tony Blair the benefit of the doubt, why did he never correct the public record or apologise for having misled Parliament? Why did his Foreign Minister fail to pass the information to Downing Street? Why did he not make any inquiries to check whether or not his Ministers had been informed about the alleged abuses? Why was Mr Blair content, either not to check the facts or content to give out false information on a matter as serious as Abu Ghraib?

# Two Fingers to Regionalisation

James Frayne

T he massive 'No' vote in the North East referendum on whether there should be an elected Regional Assembly in November 2004 was a complete shock to the Government. It was never meant to happen. From the very beginning the Government had done all it could to make sure it was a walk in the park and itscampaigns showed their willingness to do anything to try to secure victory.

For a start, the Government loaded the referendum question in favour of a yes vote by making sure the ballot paper included a preamble which claimed the new Assembly would take considerable powers from central Government, including "regional economic development". This should never have been there given that this was the biggest single issue of contention in the referendum – we argued that the Assembly would have no real power over things like economic development and that the Assembly was a White Elephant. Such a preamble was like having a "Vote Yes" sticker stuck on the ballot paper.

The Government also insisted that the referendum be an all-postal vote election despite concerns that all-postal votes were more open to fraud. This is obviously true but the advantage the Government had in an all-postal vote was that the various Yes campaigns (Yes 4 The North East, the Labour Party, the unions etc) had a much bigger and better campaigning infrastructure to make sure that postal votes could be collected and turnout raised. Many hoped that this minimised the chances of a shock result in the context of a low turnout and a small but motivated No Campaign.

So the Government made sure it started with huge built-in advantages and they continued to behave without respect for the rules. Above all Government politicians blurred the line between campaigning as Labour politicians – which was acceptable – and Government officials – which was not. This all came to a head when John Prescott briefed a front-page splash in a friendly newspaper saying that he had spoken to others in the Government and had managed to get a guarantee that they would secure more power over transport for the region after a yes vote. This was an obvious breach of the rules but the weakness of the Electoral Commission meant that nothing could be done and, as the Government knew all too well, there was nothing in it for the No Campaign to whinge about the technicalities of electoral rules when we wanted to be smashing the Government over the head on other issues.

This sort of political activity was not limited to national politicians. One local council used taxpayers' money to print 40,000 stickers to go on wheelie-bins backing a local government reorganisation that was dependent on a yes vote. This broke the rules about government bodies advertising during the election campaign and the Electoral Commission forced the council to remove the stickers later.

But councils were able to get their own back. Whilst it generally takes an eternity for council workers to get round to doing anything quickly, they were extremely efficient at forcing No Campaign supporters to remove posters and roadside banners which apparently breached some regulation or another. Council workers even went on to private land to try to remove "Politicians talk, we pay" posters. Some banners were literally removed within hours. It often felt like campaigning in Soviet Russia.

And all of this was taking place within the context of an unbelievably unpleasant campaign from New Labour's top politicians and their campaigners. As the polls began to move from yes to no, the accusations and personal attacks increased and became more vitriolic. This included the accusation that the No Campaign were "all Tories", and "Rather Arrogant Toff Southerners" ("RATS" – yes, really). It included claims that the No Campaign's businesspeople didn't have the interests of the region at heart and towards the end it predictably included the pathetic argument that the No Campaign was on the same side as the BNP, who also wanted a No vote.

The final result was staggering – the people of the North East voted by nearly 4-1 against a Regional Assembly (78-22 per cent). But the campaign was more brutal and unpleasant that most people realise. It revealed the very worst traits of this Government's senior politicians – their disregard for the public, their win-at-all-costs mentality, and their willingness to intimidate. The No vote should have marked a turning point in British politics where politicians were forced to change their behaviour. Unfortunately, it has been politics as usual ever since and it shows no signs of changing.

*James Frayne was campaign director of the North East Says No campaign and is campaign director of the TaxPayers' Alliance (www.taxpayersalliance.com).*

# Creative Accounting

Damon Lambert

The year 2001 saw the introduction of the government's Political Parties, Elections and Referendums Act. One of the conditions is that every quarter each political party has 30 days to submit a return of all the donations it received in the previous three months, rather similar to what thousands of businesses regularly do when submitting details of sales in their VAT returns.

Could Labour comply with its own simple requirement? As early as the third quarter of 2002, the Electoral Commission held meetings with Labour to discuss its non-compliance. In one quarter Labour forgot a whopping £1.8 million of donations. In late 2003 Labour got investigated but no further action was taken because "the Commission is satisfied that the Party Treasurer took all reasonable steps and exercised due diligence". The Party Treasurer, Jack Dromey, was so reasonable and diligent he never questioned how £17.9 million of general election costs got funded, and hence did not twig the existence of £14 million of loans from individuals. Labour's excuse that it was having transitional problems adopting to the new regime does not whitewash – the task of recording every donation and sending the list to the Electoral Commission could be done by any trainee accountant. Did Labour learn? Since the Electoral Commission's investigations, Labour has reported late donations in seven out of eight quarters, making it possibly the only examination whose pass rate has dropped in recent years. Curiously, most other parties have declared impermissible donations, and returned the sums to the would-be donors. In four years, Labour, by far the biggest recipient of largesse, has never declared a single 'bad' donation.

*Taxcutter, www.taxcutter.blogspot.com*

# Marxist Milibands?

Iain Dale

We all know that New Labour doesn't really approve of offshore trusts and tax loopholes. Well, that's their public position anyhow. The Chancellor of the Exchequer has been assiduous in closing inheritance loopholes, ably assisted over the last nine years by his policy assistant Ed Miliband (brother of Cabinet Minister David), now a Labour MP. Ed's and David's father Ralph Miliband, the Marxist historian and uber-Leftie died in 1994 having transferred almost all his assets, including homes in London and Oxfordshire, to his wife. Strangely, the family posthumously rewrote his will to give the two MP brothers a 20 per cent share of the family home in London, having been advised to do so by tax accountants. David first declared a "20% share of family home in London" on the MPs' Register of Interests in 2002, although it has curiously disappeared from the latest version. Ed Miliband has never registered it. The *Sunday Times* reported:

*"This scheme is called a "deed of variation" and was highlighted by the chancellor in opposition as an unacceptable way in which the wealthy avoid paying death duties. It allows people to inherit assets tax-free even if this goes against the wishes of the deceased. Had Ralph Miliband's will not been altered, David and Ed would have inherited the house (or the money raised from its sale) when their mother Marion died and would have faced a tax bill equivalent to 40% of its value. Instead they were able to cash in on their stakes when the family's four-bedroom townhouse in Primrose Hill, north London, was sold earlier in the summer. When it was sold they may have paid other taxes. The Milibands claim that the scheme was not established to reduce tax. However, leading accountants believe that such schemes always reduce inheritance tax bills. John Whiting, head of tax at Price Waterhouse Coopers, the accountancy firm, said: "The reason people use deeds of variation is to save inheritance tax. There has been speculation for years that this scheme would be closed and Labour identified it as an abuse, but it remains a legal tax-saving device."*

David Miliband has consistently refused to comment. As well he might.

*Iain Dale's Diary, www.iaindale.blogspot.com*

# New Labour Sleaze in . . .

# 2005

## Tony's Sleazeometer, 2005

17 sleazy episodes: Very Sleazy Guy

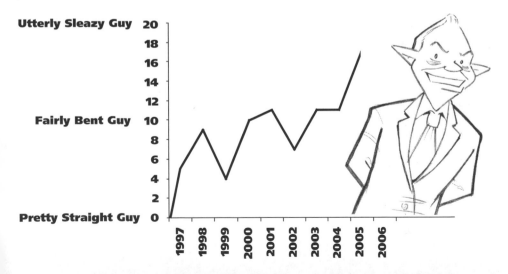

| | |
|---|---|
| **Utterly Sleazy Guy** | 20 |
| | 18 |
| | 16 |
| | 14 |
| | 12 |
| **Fairly Bent Guy** | 10 |
| | 8 |
| | 6 |
| | 4 |
| | 2 |
| **Pretty Straight Guy** | 0 |

1997 1998 1999 2000 2001 2002 2003 2004 2005 2006

# Cherie Coins it Down Under

John Angliss

It must be coincidence that Cherie Blair is mentioned so often in this book despite the powers of white witchcraft and Catholicism she has summoned to protect her. To honour this one-woman *Da Vinci Code*, the tale of her Australian speaking tour in 2005 must be told. Tickets to hear the First Lady of Downing Street cost between £75 and £4,100 and "100% of the profits" were to go to the Children's Cancer Institute Australia. An uncharacteristically generous gesture from Cherie.

Shortly afterwards, *The Times* published a draft budget which proved that this was entirely correct. The only snag was the small matter of the £102,000 of expenses which would go straight into the pockets of Cherie and her agent as a flat fee for the tour. This not only meant that those who paid out their cash for charity felt cheated, but also that the very future of the charity itself was put in jeopardy. Since only 8 per cent of gross earnings (£6,690) from the event reached the charity, it was in breach of its licence. It has since been resuscitated.

Having made enough PR mistakes during the Peter Foster/Cheriegate, it is interesting to note that Downing Street refused to comment throughout this debacle. Indeed, the whole tour turned into a PR nightmare for Cherie herself, exemplified when in New Zealand she addressed the crowds as "Australians".

According to *The Times*, a further speaking arrangement in Melbourne generated £6,774 for charity and £17,000 for the speaker. Small change for Cherie.

# Pants "Not on Fire"

Wat Tyler

Just what does it take to make your pants catch fire? Steve "Pants" Byers was determined to find out. In June 2001 he took a job as Transport Secretary and set about it. First he got his Departmental team secretly working up radical restructuring options for Railtrack, a privatised company he'd taken a fancy to.

He then forced Railtrack into administration so he could renationalise it on the cheap. Dispossessed shareholders were outraged, 50,000 of them suing him for *administrative misfeasance*, last seen in 1703.

Finally he appeared before the Commons Transport Sub-Committee and brazenly denied he'd pre-planned any of it: "Was there any discussion, theoretical or otherwise, in your Department... about the possibility of a future change in status for Railtrack, whether nationalisation, the move into a company limited by guarantee, or whatever?" Byers: "Not that I am aware of."

Terrific play. But amazingly, despite a burning sensation around his crotch, his Calvins failed to ignite – later inspection revealed only a singed gusset. Everybody was very kind and *said* he was a liar, but that's not the same as actually having blazing pants. Disillusioned, he resigned.

As it turned out, he needn't have worried. In July 2005 those angry shareholders invited him to the High Court for a grilling. And there, confronted with stacks of evidence that he'd told a monstrous porkie to the Committee, his pants finally began smoldering: "It is true to say there was work going on, so, yes, that was untrue... It was such a long time ago, I cannot remember, but it is not a truthful statement... I cannot remember the motives behind it."

"Cannot remember" – brilliant stuff. In October 2005, he finished it with a personal statement to the Commons claiming he *had* now remembered: "the commissioning of work... on future options did not represent discussions in the true meaning of that word."

The old semantics one-two: superb. He sat down in triumph, evil yellow smoke belching from his rear vent. All he needed now was official authentication from the House Standards Committee.

But, incredibly, the Committee ruled against him. Yes, he'd been "factually inaccurate". Yes, he'd done it "for political reasons". And yes, he'd been "unwise" to concoct his retrospective justification. But, no, technically, his pants were "not on fire".

This is plainly ludicrous. We all *saw* the smoke, and Pants deserves proper recognition. We demand the matter be referred to the Guinness Book of Records.

*Burning Our Money, www.burningourmoney.blogspot.com*

# Because She's Worth It

Paul Sorene

Why did you vote Labour at the 2005 General Election? Was it the Party's stance on the NHS, the war in Iraq, the leader's relationship with Cliff Richard? Or was it something else? Was it Cherie Blair's hair?

During the 2005 election campaign, the Labour Party was asked to pay £7,700 to secure the services of Cherie's personal hairstylist. The crimper's name was Andre Suard, and for £275 a day between 6th April and 6th May 2005 he strove to make Cherie look good enough to woo your vote.

Not that she was standing for Parliament – she unsuccessfully stood for Parliament in the 1980s; Cherie was applying for the job of First Lady. As Peter Kilfoyle, a backbench Labour MP, said: "We are almost accepting by stealth a First Lady."

This was nonsense. There was nothing stealthy about it. American magazines have often referred to Cherie as the first lady. She was billed as "The trail-blazing first lady of Downing Street" when on her lucrative speaking tour in the States. And Cherie did not object.

And Cherie's hair has form, to go with that 'because-I'm-worth-it bounce'. Suard has accompanied Cherie on trips to Indonesia, Australia and the United States.

Sir Christopher Meyer, Britain's former ambassador to Washington, recalled in his memoirs one brush with Cherie's stylist. "Suddenly," says Meyer, "the cry went up: Cherie's hairdresser is missing! Her French stylist had accompanied us on our mission... He had been left behind at Camp David. A US marines helicopter brought him post-haste... as the rest of us kicked our heels."

But why should we care? As a spokesman for the party told us: "So what? Mrs Blair worked fantastically hard during the election and visited more than 50 constituencies during the campaign. She is enormously popular with the party and, don't forget, we won the election." So the two things are linked. It was the hair wot won it.

Over seven grand on hair does seem a lot, but when viewed as part of the race for power, it is cheap. And represents far better value than buying, say, a peerage. As Lord Suard of Barnet can only agree.

*Anorak, www.anorak.co.uk*

" CHEAPER IN THE LONG RUN, MADAM "

# Cherie Goes to Washington

Christopher Doidge

Cherie Blair – (or Booth when it suits her) – called in to question the 'spirit' of the Ministerial Code of Conduct in June 2005, when she seemingly benefited from her role as the Prime Minister's wife to the tune of over £30,000.

Blair – sorry, Booth – claimed her trip was unrelated to her time spent as Tony's consort, yet advertised a lecture she gave in Washington as an irresistible opportunity to hear from the "First Lady of Downing Street".

It seems unlikely that a lecture given by any other well-known QC would have attracted such a crowd, nor provided a pay-check for somewhere north of £30,000. And Mrs Blair/Booth's fee didn't include the royalties she earned from her book *The Goldfish Bowl: Married to the Prime Minister 1955-1997*.

While the Ministerial Code doesn't include the spouses of Ministers, Cherie's foray into highly-paid lecturing wasn't exactly in the spirit of the rule which states that ministers "should not accept payment for speeches of an official nature or which directly draw on their responsibilities or experience".

Arguably, given that Cherie and Tony probably share a bank account, Mr Blair himself probably benefited from the speech. His defence was that Norma Major never declared how much she made from a book on the PM's official residence, Chequers.

But criticism came from all sides. Peter Kilfoyle, the Labour backbencher said he thought the rules governing MPs' conduct were being applied more strongly for those at the bottom of the 'greasy pole' than those at the top.

And although Cherie's travel costs were paid privately (well, she can just about afford it with annual earnings from Matrix Chambers of circa £250,000), the Conservatives' Chris Grayling said, "There is no doubt in my mind that the Prime Minister and Mrs Blair have broken the spirit of the rules, if not the rules themselves." But calls for reform of the Code met with little response from Number 10.

Cherie's trip coincided with a trip by her husband to the very same city, although in one of the least plausible statements ever made by the Prime Minister's Official Spokesman, reporters were told that "If she and the Prime Minister are in Washington at the same time it is a coincidence."

Controversy-prone Cherie will probably chuckle that her hefty fee (merely a small portion of the Blairs' numerous mortgages) will have brought her long-term gain at the expense of short-term sleaze.

*www.warwick.ac.uk/blogs/cdoidge*

# Cherie Blair (Not) Cutting the Ribbon

Shaun Rolfe

On 16th June 2005 the *Guardian* reported: "In a [strange] coincidence, it seems that Cherie Booth's visit next month to Kuala Lumpur, where she will deliver a law lecture and attend a breast cancer charity gala, will coincide with the relaunch of the duty free shopping complex Starhill, where the gala will take place. In preparation for this great occasion, each of the mall's seven floors has been given an enticing new name: Feast, Indulge, Adorn, Explore, Pamper, Relish and Muse.

In yet another coincidence, Starhill's owner, a Malaysian magnate called Francis Yeoh, has pointed out that the 'global arbiters of taste and style' whose shops now ornament his refurbished mall include 'Eric Way, the young and exciting couture designer, [who] dresses high-profile clients like Cherie Blair, Ivana Trump, Shirley Bassey...' As for Way, he has told a journalist that Mrs Blair will wear one of his dresses to the gala, where her fellow guests, according to the organisers, will include Dame Shirley Bassey and possibly, Ivana Trump.

As the devout Yeoh has pointed out in another context, 'All of mankind today is spun together in a complex web of interdependence. The consequence of interdependence is that we have a stake in each other's economic well-being.' Yeoh, for example, has a stake in Wessex Water. Why shouldn't Mrs Blair's visit further the interests of the Malaysian economy? Or, at least, that large part of the Malaysian economy that belongs to Yeoh's YTL conglomerate, where the guiding philosophy is: 'World Class Products and Services at Third World Prices'? No reason, except that Yeoh's business thinking is not yet universally applied, with the result that some people are asking, with even more intensity than they asked last week, if Mrs Blair has taken leave of her senses."

Ten days later a Downing Street spokesman told reporters that Cherie Blair would not now attend the opening of the shopping mall due to "scheduling issues".

"They've all been disinvited. He doesn't want any British celebrities or press there," said Eric Way, the couturier who introduced Cherie to Mr Yeoh.

At the same briefing, in what was reported as a coordinated move to end criticism of Mrs Blair's money-making, the Number 10 spokesman said that Mrs Blair would donate to charity the fee from the forthcoming Channel 4 documentary based on her book *The Goldfish Bowl*. How gracious of her.

# Play it Again, Richard

Tom Barry

Richard Bowker is an interesting example of how far a judicious bit of networking can take you. A fine pianist, in 2002, shortly after moving from Virgin Rail to head the Strategic Rail Authority, he accompanied the Prime Minister's guitar at a private birthday party. The logic of appointing someone from one of the chief trouble-makers in the rail industry, whose grandiose plans were swallowing billions of pounds of taxpayers' money, is questionable; Virgin benefited from millions in subsidy from the SRA during Bowker's reign there, paying for the extra costs associated with their new trains, which he'd ordered. These are less efficient, of lower capacity, cause more damage to the track and require more staff. The result was predictable: in 2003/4 Virgin's Cross Country franchise should have received £50 million in subsidy and falling; the reality was a cool £250 million after a steep increase as Bowker's vision took wing.

The man at the top, by now combining the Chief Executive and Chairman role, was unbowed and in another musical interlude, he sang perfectly off the same hymn sheet as Tony Blair and Alistair Darling. Over three days in mid-2003 each man made a star-tlingly similar speech blaming "long-term underinvestment" for spiralling rail costs, missing the more obvious point that the structure of the industry inevitably resulted in increased cost.

By 2004, however, a note of disharmony came in. Virgin's Cross Country franchise was effectively cancelled and taken back into State control, with Virgin managing it for a percentage of income. Bowker admitted that costs were out of control, partly because of the overruns on the West Coast scheme he had helped devise back at Virgin. The Department for Transport starting planning to throw him out of his job.

The 2005 Railways Act abolished the SRA after four years in which it had done nothing except perpetuate the inefficient and costly bureaucracy of privatisation and add its own layer. In a final twist, 150 SRA civil servants continued to turn up to work for six months after the SRA's abolition.

However, all was not lost for Richard. In the big final number of the musical, he was rewarded for the abolition of his organisation with the CBE, and for his expertise in handing out vast sums of taxpayers' money by being made Chief Executive of Partnerships for Schools, spending £40 billion of your money on school PFI deals to create Tony Blair's 'legacy'.

# The 'Terrorist' Heckler Pensioner

Tom Paine

The Walter Wolfgang incident is a small, perfect emblem of New Labour. Mr Wolfgang, an escapee from Nazism, is a long-time member of the Labour Party. He is an old-fashioned 'peace activist', more in keeping with the Party's Michael Foot epoch than with the glossy hardness of Blair and Brown. For him to frighten a fly, the insect would have to be of a rather nervous disposition. At the Labour Party's 2005 annual conference, in the best rough-and-tumble traditions of British debate, he shouted "nonsense" (or something to that effect) during a speech by the then Foreign Secretary, Jack Straw. In a rational world, he would have won a prize for staying awake in such trying circumstances and making a statement of the bleedin' obvious.

Straw is as weak an orator as he is a sex symbol (however much he wanted to be both when around Condoleeza Rice or various Blair Babes). Instead, in the irrational world we actually inhabit, Wolfgang was seized and forcibly ejected by the Party's hired thugs/security guards. So fragile is the connection between the "People's Party" and any actual people it encounters these days, the frail old geezer seems to have frightened the men of power. After his unseemly ejection, "Wolfie" (as he is known in Leftist circles) was arrested by police using "anti-terrorist" powers.

New Labour has lavished such powers on the police throughout its time in office. In theory, they are to protect us against the dark forces of terrorism. In fact, they are more to do with outflanking the Conservative Party on its traditional "safe ground" of law and order. "You want to hang them high? We will hang them higher!" (or rather fire seven head shots into them as they travel innocently to work). Libertarians have squawked in protest, but have been written off as mere "liberati" by such moral giants as David Blunkett. We warned darkly that new police powers would be used in ways that voters never imagined. Certainly, few imagined they would be used to harass frail old Labourites raising a quavering voice of dissent.

It was a tiny incident. Wolfie lives, unharmed; basking a little in his moment of fame. Blair's apology has been accepted. Too old to learn new tricks, Wolfie remains the naive socialist he has always been. But the curtain had slipped and we all had a small glimpse of our future.

*The Last Ditch, www.lastditch.blogspot.com*

# Masters of False Reality

Justin McKeating

Proof that New Labour is the greatest political party in history was presented by Channel 4's *Dispatches* on 23rd May 2005. Not content with three historic election victories, bringing democracy to Iraq and the elevation of a priapic blind man to one of the great offices of state, New Labour can conjure worlds of their own imagining from the raw firmament.

The programme showed that the party is adept at creating what *Sky News*'s Political Editor, Adam Boulton, called a "false reality".

Propaganda techniques used by US pharmaceutical companies and political parties – known as "astroturfing" – were imported. Letters written by press officers praising New Labour or attacking the opposition were sent to activists who were told to get them into the local press. Identical letters appeared in newspapers across the country. One appeared in the same newspaper twice. In Leeds, letters were printed from a woman who didn't exist.

Fake demonstrations were organised to follow the leaders of the opposition parties and disrupt walkabouts and rallies. Outside the Tory's spring conference in Brighton, New Labour activists organised what was meant to look like a "spontaneous" protest by members of the public. The 'homemade' banners made no mention of Labour affiliations. Standing front and centre in the crowd was the New Labour candidate, and now MP, for Hove, Celia Barlow.

Throughout the New Labour campaign, the national media was bypassed almost completely with only TV cameras and local press invited to events. After Blair was ambushed by Nick Robinson at a poster launch, care was taken not to let it happen again. At the next event, once the cameras had got pictures for the evening news, party workers were corralled in front of reporters to prevent them getting to Blair. He shook hands with "endorsers", people billed as "ordinary voters and a cross section of the local community". In reality they were carefully chosen (black, Jewish, pensioners, families) to present the right image. These endorsers were endlessly recycled at different events.

Adam Boulton spoke of Blair's "sterile environment". Robinson wondered whether Blair had met a single real member of the electorate during the campaign, isolated as he was, from another Sharon Storer, the distraught partner of a cancer sufferer who had accosted him during the 2001 campaign. Did Blair or Brown realise they were meeting "voters" they'd "met" at other events, some of whom were party workers? Did they know they were making small talk with people handpicked because they were telegenic or fitted an ethnic demographic?

Boulton was generous and described Blair as "above it". But Blair was only one level removed, with Alastair Campbell and Alan Milburn "high-fiving" (as a *Dispatches* undercover reporter witnessed) in the press office.

*Chicken Yoghurt, www.chickyog.blogspot.com*

# Moneygrabbing

Dizzy

Like the colour of their logo, New Labour has been in the red with their bank manager for a while. Those pre-election loans in 2005 certainly didn't help move the books into the black. The debt problems might help explain why Labour HQ decided to start charging £200 for information requests about their Prospective Parliamentary Candidates (PPCs) back in March 2005.

If you're wondering what sort of information I mean, it's basically their CVs. You know the sort of stuff, what school you went to – Fettes for example. Your experiences of real work – I stress "real". Or the other usual lies you put in CVs such as "I support Newcastle United".

Now you may very well think that this is not a major scandal. After all, £200 doesn't sound like a lot of money, but what if you were a voter who wanted to know about PPC? Suddenly you're told you need to pay for information that you have a right to know?

It's very simple, if you're going to stand for Parliament – like one of the editors of this book did – then you're entering PUBLIC life. That means you let the public know about you openly when they ask and to hell with the consequences.

The fact that Labour wanted to charge for access to this information means they were either seriously stuck for cash (possible); many of their candidates had more skeletons in their cupboards than Alan Clark (feasible); or they're just a bunch of money grabbers (likely). Or all three. You decide.

*Dizzy Thinks, http://dizzythinks.blogspot.com*

# Bullying Journalists

Iain Dale

A lastair Campbell is renowned for bullying journalists and for his foul, sleazy mouth. If we ever had any doubt about the matter, all we need do is look at the extracts from his diaries which he was forced to make public during the Hutton Inquiry. One particularly charming extract reads: "I agreed it would fuck Gilligan if that [Dr Kelly] was his source."

But an even better example came in an email containing a four-letter outburst aimed at BBC journalists. Mr Campbell sent the email by mistake to BBC2's *Newsnight* after it questioned his role in Labour's controversial campaign posters.

He later emailed the show saying the original email had been sent in error and that it was all a "silly fuss". Campbell messaged *Newsnight* after the programme investigated claims that Labour's advertising agency TBWA was blaming him for the brouhaha over its campaign posters. The images, including one of flying pigs and another of what critics claim depicted Tory leader Michael Howard as Fagin, prompted accusations of anti-Semitism. Mr Campbell's email, which was apparently intended for a party official, suggested they should get Trevor Beattie, TBWA's MD, to issue a statement.

In the email Alastair Campbell said: "Just spoke to trev. think tbwa shd give statement to newsnight saying party and agency work together well and nobody here has spoken to standard. Posters done by by tbwa according to political brief. Now fuck off and cover something important you twats!" The email was sent by mistake to *Newsnight* journalist Andrew McFadyen. Realising his error, Mr Campbell then emailed Mr McFadyen pointing out the mistake, but suggesting presenter Jeremy Paxman would have seen the funny side. He said: "Not very good at this email Blackberry malarkey. Just looked at log of sent messages, have realised email meant for colleagues at TBWA has gone to you. For the record, first three sentences of email spot on. No row between me and trevor. Posters done by them according to our brief.

I dreamt up flying pigs. Pigs not great but okay in the circs of Tories promising tax cuts and spending rises with the same money. TBWA made production. Campbell swears shock. Final sentence of earlier email probably a bit colourful and personal considering we have never actually met but I'm sure you share the same sense of humour as your star presenter Mr P. Never known such a silly fuss since the last silly fuss but there we go. Must look forward not back." Indeed we must.

*Iain Dale's Diary, www.iaindale.blogspot.com*

# The Union Modernisation Fund

Matthew Sinclair

L abour is facing a fairly serious funding crisis. Thanks to this crisis it is dependent upon the generous support of the unions. Unfortunately the unions aren't rolling in cash either. Their membership has been in decline for some time as people move out of highly unionised industries and into the service sector. It is at precisely this moment when the whole house of loan-slips threatens to come crashing down that the Union Modernisation Fund, a vehicle for the Labour government to give £10 million of taxpayer money to the unions over three years, is created. Such a coincidence makes people cynical. The department responsible for the plan, the Department of Trade and Industry, makes clear that this money cannot be used for political projects. Unfortunately, the unions, like most organisations, have limitations on their budget and their membership's willingness to pay expanded dues. If the Government is willing to pay for Amicus to communicate with its branches then more of the income that comes from its members is likely to be sent the Labour Party's way. It is for this reason that Frances Maude called this plan "very, very direct sleaze. That is buying influence and buying taxpayers' money". The Metropolitan Police are apparently investigating.

Some of the scheme's supporters counter that, as money is also given to unions who do not fund the Labour Party, this is not a scheme designed to reward supporters. Unfortunately, all that suggests is that the Labour Party doesn't mind spreading taxpayer money around a little in order to make the sleaze a little less brutally obvious.

The decline of the unions is a process which places the Labour Party in crippling financial difficulties thanks to the Party's inability to raise funds from an increasingly disillusioned membership. That it is intervening and providing government support to a lobby group which acts only in its own interests rather than the national interest is a scandal. It is of course a clear 'result' for trade union and Labour Party treasurers.

*Sinclair's Musings, http://sinclairsmusings.blogspot.com*

# It Pays to Talk

Guido Fawkes

The Official Labour Election Night Party in May 2005, held at the National Portrait Gallery, and organised by PR guru Matthew Freud, at a cost of £50,000 (paid for personally by Charlie Dunstone, the Carphone Warehouse multi-millionaire). It was attended by Lord Levy, the Labour fundraiser. David Campbell, chief executive of the Anschutz Entertainment Group was another guest. He is now set to make millions by bringing gambling to the Millennium Dome, thanks to Labour's relaxing of the gaming laws. The takeover of the disastrous Dome was itself politically controversial, with allegations flying about of influence peddling.

Charles Dunstone, chief executive of Carphone Warehouse, claimed the Labour Party tried to bounce him into making a £1m donation. Dunstone, who is a fan of Tony Blair but not of Labour, said he was "nobbled" by Lord Levy, the party's sleazy fundraiser.

"I saw Lord Levy walk past me," said the owner of Talk Talk "Then he spun round, came back and said: 'You are Charles Dunstone, aren't you?' I said yes. He said: 'Good. Can we put you down for a million?'" Dunstone tried to brush off the "extraordinary" comment but the ever persistent man dubbed "Lord Cashpoint" eventually extracted his business card from him. The centi-millionaire founder of the mobile phone giant admitted that Lord Levy's flippant approach was serious. Dunstone later wrote to the party's general secretary expressing his outrage at the approach, saying he has no plans to donate money to Labour or any other party. "I don't feel comfortable doing it and I think if you're a person closely associated with any business it's a bad thing to do. It's bad to align your organisation with a political organisation." Charlie Dunstone knew better than to risk repelling his millions of individual customers by becoming notorious as a Labour-backing business tycoon, or possibly since his business does not rely on government contracts or influence, he was immune to Lord Levy's charming menace.

*www.order-order.com*

# Candy Atherton's Opposition 'Research'
Simon Maybin

The folk in deepest Cornwall are not famed for their open-mindedness. So when Paul Phillips, researcher for the Labour MP for Falmouth & Camborne Candy Atherton, felt he was being asked by his employer to "look into" stories about the local Tory candidate's gay lifestyle, Phillips was understandably uncomfortable.

It didn't help matters that Phillips himself was openly gay, and felt he was expected to use his 'insider knowledge' of the London scene to dig up some dirt.

Candy Atherton told Phillips of a press story she had seen about Ashley Crossley. She recounted the tale – laughing as she told it, according to Phillips – of how Crossley had been held at knifepoint. Atherton, Phillips alleged, wanted her researcher to find out more. He walked out.

Phillips brought an employment tribunal claim against Atherton for discrimination and harassment on the grounds of sexual orientation. At the hearing Atherton admitted asking her researcher to find out about Crossley, her Tory opponent, but said she "would not want any personal political gain because of other people's prejudice".

The claim was eventually thrown out because it had been made too late, although the panel also said it did not accept parts of Phillips's story.

Of course being a journo by trade, Candid Candy could have had no idea how these kinds of revelations would have played with the Cornwall electorate. On her website – under the heading 'Family Life' – Atherton happily informs readers that in 2001 she "married her long-term partner, Cornishman Broderick Ross".

As it turned out, the publicity wasn't great for either candidate come the general election. Atherton was booted out by LibDem media 'dahling' Julia Goldsworthy in the May 2005 vote. Crossley, who had also suffered from some vicious homophobia at the hands of his local constituency party, came a close third.

# Labour and Unison Breach Electoral Laws in Unison?

Damon Lambert

It's hard to know quite where the Labour Party ends and Unison begins. As Gordon Brown said after the 2005 general election: "I thank UNISON because, under Dave Prentis' leadership, and with the campaign you mounted, the national posters warning of the threat of the Tory party; the 300,000 direct mailings that you sent to people in key constituencies; the trade union co-ordinators you provided in 43 of the key seats that we were fighting; and the vital work you did targeting these marginals; without your work, we would not have won. That is why I am so grateful to you."

According to the Electoral Commission's records, UNISON donations to Labour during the election were £24,493. Staff costs were £6,707. If UNISON provided 43 staff then they must have paid on average £155 for over four weeks' work. What a scandal, UNISON does not even pay minimum wage! If the rest of the donation is assumed to be the 300,000 direct mailings then UNISON must be congratulated on going to the post office and managing to buy 300,000 rare six-pence stamps, with presumably a whole load of paper, envelopes and printing ink chucked in for free.

Section 50 of the the Political Parties, Elections and Referendums Act ("PPERA") considers donations to include any paying of expenses incurred directly or indirectly by the party, the provision otherwise than on commercial terms of any property, services or facilities for the use or benefit of the party (including the services of any person). Examples are shown clearly in the guidelines.

As Gordon Brown is meant to be a stickler for detail may be his Labour Party colleagues would like to bear in mind the relevant section of the PPERA.:

*Section 61. – (1) A person commits an offence if he-*
*(a knowingly enters into, or*
*(b knowingly does any act in furtherance of, any arrangement which facilitates or is likely to facilitate, whether by means of any concealment or disguise or otherwise, the making of donations to a registered party by any person or body other than a permissible donor*

*Taxcutter, www.taxcutter.blogspot.com*

# The Second Resignation of David Blunkett MP

Gregor Hopkins

D avid Blunkett's second resignation illustrates just how far removed from reality long-serving Cabinet Ministers can become. They think they're omnipotent. They believe whatever they do they can get away with. They become remote from the 'little people' as their ministerial Jaguars shuttle them from pillar to post. But events catch up with them in the end and it is in this light that we must view Blunkett's second ignoble resignation.

The circumstances leading up to 'second resignation' day on 2nd November 2005 are well documented. A year previously he had left Blair's Cabinet in disgrace over 'Nannygate' and was continuing his public spat with ex-mistress Kimberly Quinn over their illegitimate child. Perhaps it is understandable that Mr B took his eye off the ball and went onto achieve his spectacular 'double'.

In March 2005 the one-time leading socialist and hater of capitalism David Blunkett bought shares in DNA Biosciences and was made a non-executive director of the company. In itself this posed no problem and shouldn't have caused any eyebrows to be raised unduly. But following the 2005 election Tony Blair decided to appoint Blunkett to be Secretary of State for Work & Pensions, a Department in which DNA Biosciences was bidding for lucrative contracts. If those contracts came to fruition Blunkett stood to make a shed load of money. The problem was that David Blunkett hadn't registered his directorships properly.

Unfortunately, a grey area in the parliamentary system is that following the dissolution of Parliament, prior to a General Election, the country has no Parliament and no MPs. Therefore, strictly speaking, Blunkett didn't need to register his little money spinner. Although he did let it be known that he had bought the shares, he didn't register them with the Cabinet Secretary at the time. Furthermore, and perhaps fatally for his career, he didn't respond to any of the three (yes, three) letters from the Advisory Committee on Business Appointments which advised him to seek committee approval for his venture.

Though warned that these shares presented a startling conflict of interest, Blunkett soldiered on – a bit of fobbing here, a declaration of innocence there. But in the end it all caught up with him. Sir Alistair Graham, chairman of the Committee on Standards in Public Life proclaimed that he had breached the ministerial code, which in effect meant the game was up. He handed in his resignation but from his subsequent statements you could tell he couldn't quite see what he had done wrong. The whole episode left one with a distinct feeling of déjà vu.

*The Travelblog, www.gregor.org.uk*

# Taking Liberties

Jonathan Sheppard

The Labour Government is full of contradiction with this fact being most apparent in the area of civil liberties. On the one hand they have singularly failed to stamp down on anti-social behaviour, yet at the same time they have presided over the biggest erosion of civil liberties of the law-abiding majority ever seen in the history of our country. The Government suggests ID cards are required for the war against terrorism, yet who could trust a Labour Government whose control freakery in the past has led to an 82-year-old heckler, Walter Wolfgang, being ejected from the Labour Conference, and one of their own MPs, Austin Mitchell, having his camera seized and his pictures deleted.

More recently this constant obsession at controlling our lives led to a 25-year-old vegan cook from Hastings being found guilty of breaching Section 132 of the new Serious Organised Crime and Police Act. She was arrested in October for reading names of soldiers killed in Iraq at central London's Cenotaph.

What does this tell us about the country we live in? Don't disagree – because if you do they will introduce a law which makes it illegal. Don't protest – or you could go to jail. Don't go off message, even if you are a Labour MP – or suffer the consequences. Civil liberties have to be protected, but Labour sees them as just another added complication whose erosion is a price worth paying. Is this sleaze? Surely the curtailment of freedom of speech using legislation which we were promised would never be used improperly is the ultimate betrayal.

*Tory Radio, www.toryradio.com*

# New Labour Sleaze in . . .

# 2006

## Tony's Sleazeometer, 2006

20 sleazy episodes: Utterly Sleazy Guy (and that's just up to May!)

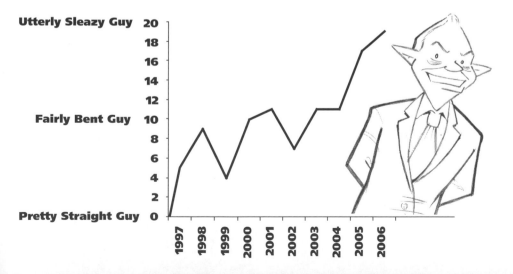

# An 'Inadvertent Error'

Bel Andrew

Until his recent fall from grace, the Deputy Prime Minister, John Prescott, was the Cabinet minister in charge of council tax. Taxpayers are struggling under the rising burden of this most unfair of local taxes. Pensioners on fixed incomes are among the hardest hit. Annual council tax increases outstrip the rate of inflation. Appeals for relief fall on deaf ears, and pensioners are being jailed for non-payment. Not all tax-dodging old people are treated in this way, though.

It was revealed in January 2006 that 67-year-old Prescott had not paid a single council tax bill since 1997 for his plush grace-and-favour flat in Admiralty Arch. The taxpayer paid his total bill of £3,830.52. He says it was all a mistake, an "inadvertent error" by his staff. Poor lamb. He thought that the tax was deducted along with his income tax. Since when is council tax collected through PAYE? Perhaps somebody (a real pensioner, maybe) could try that defence in court: "Sorry m'lud, I thought my council tax had been deducted from my already meagre pension", etc. Anyway, since when was ignorance of the law a defence?

In addition the flat was incorrectly classed as his "secondary" residence, thereby qualifying for a discount. So the actual tax due should have been much higher than £3,830.52. Mr Prescott again claimed ignorance, blaming this on the previous Conservative administration.

He has promised to refund the money, and ordered that future bills be sent directly to him. Perhaps a little late.

*Bel is Thinking, www.declaim.blogspot.com*

# Margaret Beckett's Air Miles

Andrew Woodman

Margaret Beckett is the ex-Bennite ex-deputy leader of the Labour Party, ex-Secretary of State at the Department of the Environment and now our first female and first caravanning Foreign Secretary.

When she was Secretary of State for the Environment, her department's website stated: "Mrs Beckett leads for the UK in international negotiations on sustainable development and climate change" She was therefore, the Government leader on 'going green'.

Reconcile this with the admission that Margaret Beckett took 106 RAF flights between 2002 and December 2004 whilst in that role. Yes, to travel the 130 miles between the DEFRA office to the city of Derby, the woman in charge of the Environment rejected the train (station three miles from her home) and instead took the RAF Squadron 32 to East Midlands Airport (13 miles away from her home). The monetary cost of all this being allegedly only a notional £107,000. The National Audit Office estimates the actual cost to be more like £1m. A shocking use and waste of public money. One wonders how she tipped the pilot.

However, it doesn't end there. Consider this report from the BBC: "The UK is unlikely to meet its target of reducing $CO_2$ emissions by 20% by 2010, a Government report says. 'The Climate Change Programme review projects that new and existing policies will deliver a cut of 15-18% by the end of the decade. Environment Secretary Margaret Beckett said the government was not giving up on meeting the 20% goal, but said more had to be done to reach it. The review encourages people to cut their personal emissions.'"

Will she practise what she used to preach now she is Foreign Secretary? A nation waits to find out.

*Reinstate Roger Helmer, www.reinstateroger.com*

# Fancy a Peerage, Boyo?

Peter Henn

Blaenau Gwent was the seat Labour would never lose. A seat held, in various incarnations, by Nye Bevan and Michael Foot. So, in 2005, Labour promptly lost it. The local Labour Party wanted Assembly Member and former council leader Peter Law to replace Llew Smith. The national Labour Party announced they weren't going to listen to BGCLP and insisted on having an all-woman shortlist, much to the chagrin of many local members, who promptly tore up their membership cards in protest. Now, were you a Labour supporter, who would you trust? The people who gave Parliament the likes of Bevan and Foot, or the people who decided that Ron Davies, the badger's friend, should be put in charge of Wales?

After wrestling with his conscience Peter Law decided to stand against the official Labour candidate and to everyone's astonishment he overturned a Labour majority of 19,000 with a majority of his own of more than 9,000.

It was too good to last. In April 2006 Mr Law, who in the meantime had become one of the most popular constituency MPs in the country, lost his battle with cancer. Before he was even buried, Labour HQ had started canvassing for the coming by-election.

A week after his death Peter Law's widow Trish gave an interview to the Welsh political programme *Dragon's Eye*. She duly announced that a "senior" Labour figure had offered her husband a peerage if he agreed not to stand in the election. The Labour Party press machine swung into action and immediately denied any wrongdoing. A week later, on local election polling day, Plaid Cymru leader Elfyn Llwyd MP accused Welsh Secretary Peter Hain of doing the dirty deed. Even worse for Labour, he alleged under the cloak of parliamentary privilege that it had all happened with the authority of the Prime Minister.

A postscript: Maggie Jones was given a peerage in the 2006 Honours list, no doubt for "services to the Labour Party". She had contrived to lose the safest Labour seat in Wales. Makes you long for an elected second chamber, doesn't it?

# Red Ken's Standards Found Wanting

Andrew Ian Dodge

On 24th February 2006 London Mayor Ken Livingston lost his appeal against suspension by The Adjudication Panel for England when they upheld the Board of Deputies of British Jews' complaint, that Ken comparing an *Evening Standard* reporter, Oliver Feingold, to a "concentration camp guard" brought his office into disrepute. To quote the panel which passed the one-month ban (on full pay): "The case tribunal is, however, concerned that the Mayor does seem to have failed, from the outset of this case, to have appreciated that his conduct was unacceptable, was a breach of the code [the GLA code of conduct] and did damage to the reputation of his office."

They went on to say it was "unnecessarily insensitive and offensive".

Ken and his supporters protested, believing that the voters of London were the only ones able to remove him from the office of Mayor. The exchange between the Mayor and the *Evening Standard* reporter occurred outside a party celebrating the twentieth anniversary of Chris Smith, former Islington MP, declaring his homosexuality. The exchange was caught on tape which was played to the panel and widely distributed in both the media and online.

Ken Livingstone was recorded asking reporter Oliver Feingold if he is a "German war criminal". Mr Feingold replies: "No, I'm Jewish, I wasn't a German war criminal. I'm quite offended by that." The mayor then says: "Ah right, well you might be, but actually you are just like a concentration camp guard, you are just doing it because you are paid to, aren't you?"

Despite having written for the *Evening Standard* as a restaurant critic the Mayor excused his comments as being about the record of newspaper's owner, Associated Newspapers, during the 1930s. He felt their record during the 1930s justified his description of one of their reporters.

Ken's supporters reacted angrily to the ruling. Sir Iqbal Sacranie, the Secretary

General of the Muslim Council of Britain, said: "This decision constitutes a clear over-reaction and an affront to our democratic traditions."

The ruling and four-week suspension from office – at the time of writing still subject to a judicial review brought by Livingstone – tarnished the Mayor's reputation for being welcoming and embracing to all of London's ethnic communities. The jibe was one of a string of dubious comments and behaviour regarding Jews in London. But, incredibly, such statements did not stop with the ruling – he has since made dubious comments about the Reuben brothers, who are Jewish, and their reluctance to sell land he wants for the 2012 Olympic project.

*Dodgeblogium, www.andrewiandodge.com*

# Loans for Lordships

Jonathan Sheppard and Guido Fawkes

In the spring of 2006 Blair's credibility with the public fell to new depths when the "Loans for Lordships" scandal hit the front pages and Scotland Yard launched a criminal investigation into political corruption. On a little-read blog belonging to Nick Bowes, the Labour Party's former Head of High Value Fundraising, he wrote on 21st March that "I have been minded to write an explosive entry about millionaire loans to the Labour Party for a while now".

The explosive entry, if it were ever to be written would have admitted that the serious allegations about loans being made to the Labour Party in return for seats in the House of Lords had substance. If it was an opposition politician making this allegation it would be written off as a party political spat, but when a former Labour staffer, an associate of Lord Levy, Blair's personal fundraiser, states on his own blog that "the whole peerages thing is corrupt", then questions have to be asked. Indeed Scotland Yard detectives are asking the questions of Lord Levy, the man nicknamed "Mr Cashpoint".

In the run-up to the last election the Labour Party secured loans of £14 million from wealthy business people including £1 million from Rod Aldridge, CEO of Capita. Capita is a firm with *billions* in government contracts so would be vulnerable to an approach from the Prime Minister's fundraiser. We all know you "do not to ask for credit because refusal often offends". What businessman would want to offend his biggest customer, even if as the Labour Party claims it was unlikely to make any real difference, would you as CEO want to risk offending the source of more than half your revenues? Rod Aldridge didn't approach Labour with an offer to help, they approached him – "The Labour Party came to me last year in need of financial support following the costs incurred at the last general election," he said. Businessmen are cynical about politicians, most would view such an approach as a shakedown, but what real choice would they have?

Two million pounds from Richard Caring, £1.5 million from Dr Chai Patel and £2 million from David Sainsbury, the Science minister who is reputed to have lent and given over £13 million to Labour. Lord Drayson, another Government minister, got his peerage weeks after giving £500,000 to Labour. Whilst there is nothing intrinsically wrong in loaning a political party money, there is certainly something wrong if it could be seen to be buying a seat in the legislature, so much so that Nick Bowes, who worked at the heart of the Labour Party, wrote, "I still think the crucial questions are a) why were donors persuaded to change their donations into loans and b) to what extent was the Prime Minister involved? In answer to a) you have to conclude it is because they were going to get peerages and Number 10 didn't want to draw a relationship between the two and b) the Prime Minister was in it up to his neck and was personally involved."

Are we to believe that the millions loaned were given in the expectation that there was nothing to come in return? Seventeen out of 22 individuals who have recently donated over £100,000 to Labour have been given an honour, and all but one who have donated more than £1 million has been given a peerage. Unsurprisingly, a YouGov poll showed 56 per cent of people believe Tony Blair gave peerages in exchange for loans and donations.

Barry Townsley made a loan of £1 million and was recommended for the Lords. Sir David Gerrard, a property developer, loaned the party around £2 million before he was put on the list for a peerage. Sleazy Levy, who mixes in the same social circles, would have known that they were risking hundreds of millions on a development getting Government planning approval from John Prescott, Gerrard would therefore be vulnerable to an approach from the Labour Party's fundraiser – well, if you have a £600 million property development resting on Government approval what is a £3 million "loan"? Both peerages were blocked by the Lord's Appointments Commission. Des Smith, a former council member of the Specialist Schools and Academies Trust (SSA Trust), which helps the Government to recruit sponsors for Blair's academies, told an undercover *Sunday Times* reporter that big financial donations to help set up the schools would guarantee a gong. He put it plainly: "the prime minister's office would recommend someone like [the donor] for an OBE, a CBE or a knighthood".

Asked if this would be just for getting involved in the academies, he responded: "Yes ... they call them services to education. I would say to [the SSA Trust] office that we've got to start writing to the Prime Minister's office... you could go to the House of Lords". Des Smith's admission is *prima facie* evidence of what we all know. If you wanted a peerage, a seven-figure loan to the Labour Party and the same again donated to a city academy obtained it. Levy induced it. He covertly procured the money for the Labour Party.

Labour MP Austin Mitchell said "In the last election Tony panicked as usual... called Levy and said 'Get what it takes'. Which he did because he's brilliant at fund raising, So he went out on auto-beg and collected squillions for our first PFI election. Labour spent the lot (or rather chucked it away) and no one knew what was involved until now. Pity the bastard was so dependent on teenage geniuses..."

You have to ask why did the Labour Party treasurer Jack Dromey and other elected party officials know nothing about what was going on. It will be left to Deputy Assistant Commissioner John Yates, who is conducting a police investigation, to find out.

Tony Blair says he is delighted that business people support Labour. The rest of us, including his own MPs and former party workers, are left wondering why they do so.

*Tory Radio, www.toryradio.com; Guido Fawkes, www.order-order.com*

# Cameron Mackintosh's Nightmare
UKpaul

I n April 2006 the press reported that theatre magnate Cameron Mackintosh had been offered a peerage in return for a loan – an offer he very quickly refused. The stuff of which nightmares are made…

As he reflected on the offer of a Lordship in return for his loan to the Labour Party Cameron Mackintosh drifted off into sleep and into a dream ballet resembling one of his most popular productions. In that halfway house between wakefulness and oblivion there he stood, as the boy who asked for more, confronted by the looming figure of an elegantly coiffured man in a grey suit. "Please sir, all I want is a safer, cleaner West End," pleaded young Mackintosh. The man responded, with nary a mention of the problem of attracting theatregoers, but by breaking out into a lusty rendition of 'Lords for sale, going cheap, only a million quid". Surprised by this generous and unexpected offer but aware of its dubious legality Mackintosh backed away and escaped down Shaftesbury Avenue, dodging the dancing chimney sweeps and costermongers as best he could. As he passed through a deserted Whitehall he was observed by a sinister, shadowy figure who, as he passed, intoned that the only thing that counted in life was to have large amounts in the bank. Frightened that his pocket was in danger of being well and truly picked, and shocked that his charitable instincts were being compromised, he ran and hid in the shadow of the Palace of Westminster. There, at last, he found a welcoming face, "My name's Prescott," it said, "but people know me better as the 'Artless Bodger'". In their ensuing conversation Mackintosh related how he didn't expect anything in return for his generosity. "Are you daft? Everyone has their finger in the pies, even me and I ate most of mine!" "You want more?" Bodger said, "You've come to the right place."

Mackintosh jolted awake, the nightmare vision of a world where everything was tied to personal advancement fading quickly and thankfully away. The telephone rang soon after, the voice on the other end asking, "So how does Lord Mackintosh sound to you then?" The click of the receiver being replaced told that caller all he needed to know.

# John Reid Goes to Pot

Iain Dale

What with John Prescott's affair, Charles Clarke's prisoner troubles and Patricia Hewitt being booed by nurses it was hard to believe that Tony Blair's May Day week could get any worse. But it did. Scottish Police announced they had discovered a small amount of cannabis in the home of the then Defence Secretary, Dr John Reid, during a regular security sweep.

In a bizarre coincidence Reid was in Afghanistan at the time of the discovery. The police helpfully made clear that the cannabis could have been there for up to 20 years, thereby casting nasty aspersions on Mrs Reid's cleaning habits. The 'pot' was discovered in the guest room so Reid was conveniently able to make clear it must have belonged to someone else. The cannabis was said to weigh a gram and was worth 85p – that's £29 an ounce in real money. No explanation was given about the circumstances of the find. If it had been there for 20 years, why hadn't it been found before?

Were they going through the Reid sock drawer or was a sniffer dog being used? If it was a dog it must have been a very talented one because different dogs are used to find drugs and explosives. Dr Reid was very lucky indeed that the news was dominated by Prescott and Clarke. No one thought about what would happen to a serving soldier if cannabis was discovered in his house. It can safely be said that it would not be 'laughed off'. Six days later Dr Reid was promoted to the position of Home Secretary, where he now overseas our drugs policy. You couldn't make it up.

*Iain Dale's Diary, www.iaindale.blogspot.com*

# Rachel From North London

Chris Palmer

So just what does the Labour Party believe is an insult? Is it being accused of "sexing up" a dossier claiming that weapons of mass destruction could be used by Saddam Hussein in "45 minutes," or perhaps someone calling Tony Blair a liar, or even newspapers labelling the Labour Government "corruption and malicious"?

No, according to the Labour Party, these are just "false allegations" or "fabrications of the truth" (and Labour should know – they specialise in producing what many might label as lies, themselves). But no. In actual fact, according to our former Home Secretary Charles Clarke, this is an insult: "Congratulations on fixing the meeting so that nobody can ask questions! Well, I have a question. My daughter was feet away from the 7/7 King's Cross bomb, and she and some other survivors have said they are not angry with the bombers, but with the Government, because there was no public enquiry. Why is there no public enquiry?" To this spectacularly "insulting" question, Charles Clarke snarled, "Get away from me. I will not be insulted by you, this is an insult." Rachel from North London, the survivor of the King's Cross bombing and daughter of the questioner above commented, "Why is it an insult when the father of a bomb survivor, a gentle man of God, who has never caused trouble in his life, asks for a public enquiry? Why is his question not answered?" Indeed, why is this question unanswered and why was it so insulting? Is it because the question is unanswerable and asked in a rude or insulting manner? Or is it because like so many Labour Government ministers, Charles Clarke believes that his authority and word are infallible, and that those who seek to question his divine decisions are attempting to undermine and lessen his greatness?

To be fair to him, in the end Charles Clarke agreed to meet Rachel and her father and apologised to them, but Rachel is far from happy. Read about her experience at www.rachelnorthlondon.blogspot.com

*Political Crossroads, www.politicalcrossroads.blogspot.com*

# Tessa Jowell

Chris Mounsey

In early April 2006 a row erupted over the repayment of a mortgage taken out by Tessa Jowell, Minister for Culture, and her husband, international tax lawyer David Mills.

Four years before, the two had taken out a joint mortgage of £400,000 which was then paid off within a matter of weeks, apparently with the aid of a $600,000 (£344,000) gift from what Mr Mills described to his accountant as "B's people". This was assumed to refer to the then Italian Prime Minister, Silvio Berlusconi, for whom Mills had recently given favourable testimony in an alleged corruption case.

So, not only was the gift itself slightly suspect, but the way in which the gift had been dealt with raised more than an eyebrow. Tessa found herself under fire, and the explanation she offered was the most incredible part of the whole affair.

Tessa maintained ignorance of the gift and, more surprising still, was apparently unaware that the mortgage been paid off.

That this assertion was treated with a certain amount of incredulity was most certainly not at all surprising. Despite her oh-so-onerous workload, the idea that Tessa had failed to spot the lack of mortgage statements for four years, as well as the concomitant pile of vital paperwork that would have arrived – addressed both to her and her husband – upon completion of the mortgage, seemed, frankly, a little far-fetched.

Tessa's case was referred, under the Ministerial Code, to the Cabinet Secretary, Sir Gus O'Donnell, who cleared her of any wrongdoing: "The important thing is that Tessa Jowell has accepted that he [her husband] should have done [told her about the money], has said she would have informed her permanent secretary if he had done so and explained the circumstances... By the time that she became aware that it had been reclassified as earnings he was paying tax on it and therefore under the rules it did not have to be declared if it is earnings which are being taxed."

Clear? Tessa meanwhile became the first Cabinet Minister to resign from her marriage to spend more time with her job.

*Devil's Kitchen, http://blog.devilskitchendesign.com*

"YOU LOOK DIFFERENT TODAY DAVID. HAVE YOU DONE SOMETHING WITH YOUR HAIR?"

# The Tale of Two Shags and His Cocktail Sausage

Dipesh Palana

D on Juan, Casanova and Lord Byron are all names not usually linked with that of John Prescott. Although once described as an "inveterate macho", the image of a smooth, suave, sophisticated, serial seducer is scarcely compatible with the reality of the pugnacious corpulent bruiser of a Deputy Prime Minister, champion of the Labour working class, renowned for his mangled syntax and a seemingly resolute tendency to wind up with his foot in his mouth. All of that was to change in arguably Labour's worst week in office since the election of May '97.

In the week prior to the local government elections of April 2006, Labour was already facing catastrophe. Patricia Hewitt had been jeered by the Royal College of Nurses for claiming that the NHS had seen its best ever year, and Charles Clarke was close to resignation over his department's accidental release and subsequent loss of a then unknown number of dangerous foreign criminals. Westminster watchers could barely contain their delight then when the *Daily Mirror* revealed Prescott's affair with his diary secretary, 43-year-old Tracey Temple.

Almost immediately, a near torrent of other names came forward. Sarah Bissett-Scott claimed to have had a two year affair with Prescott some years previously, and allegations of several other potentially explosives affairs had yet to be confirmed at the time of writing. Tricia McDaid claimed to have been sexually harassed as a party aide and air stewardess Helga Forde claimed that her skin had crawled when Prescott ogled her breasts and said "lovely pair" as she served him fruit on a transatlantic flight. Linda McDougall, wife of MP Austin Mitchell, made allegations of having been groped as far back as 1978.

Particular mirth was had from rumours that Prescott, upon hearing that one of the affairs was to be reported, confessed to his wife Pauline first, but admitted to the wrong affair entirely. It was later revealed that had Prescott not caved in and admitted to the *Mirror*'s initial allegations, they would have had a difficult time running with the story due to a lack of credible evidence. The affairs were particularly embarrassing given Prescott's previous pious stance on ethics and morality when criticising affairs by Conservative MPs in the Major years.

Prescott faced further problems when Ms Temple, with the help of PR guru Max Clifford, sold her story to the *Mail on Sunday*, giving a tearful television interview in the process. Questions were tabled in the Commons over a possible misuse of public finances when Prescott was found to have entertained Ms Temple at his official residence, and there was much consternation over the fact that Ms Temple was being paid out of the public purse, leading to a clear conflict of interest. Although the issue had struck a chord with voters on doorsteps, and despite being denounced by female Labour MPs, with Geraldine Smith accusing him of "the worst sort of abuse of power", he refused to resign and Blair refused to fire him.

Following the allegations in the *Mail on Sunday*, Prescott threatened to take the newspaper to the Press Complaints Commission. This was seen as unwise in many quarters, not least because he had in the past year referred to the chairman of the PCC, Sir Christopher Meyer, as a "red socked fop". Further damaging revelations showed that in fact the paper had been kind to Prescott by toning down the initial story, saying off the record that the original would have been "unsuitable for a family newspaper". This didn't stop blogger Iain Dale from leaking the unflattering details of the pulled story, which were then printed in the *Sun* on local election polling day. They involved Prescott's use of Viagra, which didn't always work, a comparison of the size of his appendage to a cocktail sausage, and Prescott's predilection for being naked and engaging in sexual relations within his office with the door open, as civil servants worked around them.

The accumulation of scandals led to Labour's worst local election showing for over 30 years. Although Blair went on to purge his Cabinet in a reshuffle the following day, Prescott somehow managed to cling on to the position of Deputy Prime Minister, thus keeping the trappings of a Cabinet Minister, But was stripped of all ministerial responsibilities. The decision was criticised from both sides of the Commons, and it is suspected that a deal was struck in which Prescott would acknowledge his role and shoulder some of the burden of Labour's electoral failure. It prompted the *Sun* to run with the headline "Now we're all being screwed by Prescott!" Ms Temple wasn't so lucky. For breaching civil service rules by going public with her story, she faced being dismissed from her job.

Prescott's new image as a sexual predator was, however, sealed, as was his link with cocktail sausages. Rumour has it that several deliveries of prime English sausages were made to his offices at the Commons. Whether Prescott accepted them is unknown.

# David Mills and Aircraft to Iran

Mark Williams

David Mills, the husband of Tessa Jowell, Secretary of State for Culture, Media and Sport, is well known for his dealings with the billionaires Silvio Berlusconi and Bernie Ecclestone, but the exploits that would have really set Nye Bevan and Keir Hardie spinning in their graves were his attempted dealings with Iran.

Aircraft finance is a complicated business, and Mills was not noted for his expertise in that area, so it was perhaps surprising when he was approached in early 2002 by an Iranian businessman, Mohammed Zolanvari, a trader operating in Dubai with strong connections at the heart of the Iranian government, and in particular with former president Rafsanjani. The Rafsanjani family is one of the richest in Iran with wide interests in Kerman province, including the local airline Mahan Air, which had often benefited from preferential treatment over the ailing state airlines, Iran Air and Iran Aseman. The Iranians had agreed to buy several used Airbus aircraft from Turkish Airlines and needed to raise finance for them, although Zolanvari had agreed to underwrite the purchase. In 2002 and 2003, the Iranians raised the required finance in the London banking market and Mills acted as their lawyer in completing the transactions.

Selling aircraft to Iran is fraught with problems, not least because of a US embargo that prevents the sale of aircraft to Iran with more than 10 per cent US manufactured content. Since almost all large modern aircraft have engines or avionics made in the US it was very difficult to avoid the embargo. The aircraft from Turkish Airlines were not caught because the US parts were exported before the date of the embargo in 1995, but following a number of fatal crashes in Iran, the Iranian government ordered airlines to only buy aircraft less than five years old. This was a problem for Mills and his friends, who had been approached by an UK-based Iranian broker who offered them a deal on 12 new and used RJ-146 aircraft from British Aerospace. BAe was not likely to jeopardise its substantial US defence business by exporting embargoed aircraft to Iran, but were keen to sell the last production aircraft before they shut their commercial aviation business. Mills suggested a solution. He would speak to Baroness Symons, the Foreign Office Minister, asking for her help in smoothing the deal with the US authorities. Jowell and Mills were guests at a dinner party at Oxford given by Vernon Bogdanor, professor of politics and government at Brasenose College. Mills sat next to Baroness Symons and talked to her about his problem. Ten days later he wrote to her asking for advice. Symons responded that she had been in touch with the British embassy in Washington and had not had a favourable response, but she was available for further help if required.

Mills initially claimed that Jowell's permanent secretary had been informed, but he later admitted that this was not the case. When contacted later he said: "I have checked. I have not disclosed the fact that I work for an Iranian group because it doesn't infringe on her department at all." Mills also denied that he had been offered further assistance by Symons, but when the *Observer* published Symons' response in January 2005, this was shown to be untrue, and indeed two months later, the Baroness announced her retirement from the Government even though she was only in her early fifties.

Mills' claim that his work did not infringe on his wife's department somehow missed the point. As Secretary of State for Culture, Jowell was one of three ministers who attended regular meetingts to approve proposed exports to dubious countries such as Iran. After her husband's involvement with Iran became known, the policy ministerial review of Iranian exports was changed to a review by senior civil servants. The Government claimed this had nothing to do with Mills, but it was a curious change of policy in view of the increased security risks in the region. In 2006 the government disclosed that as a consequence of Mr Mills' business interests, Ms Jowell had been excluded from Cabinet papers and talks on Iran since 2003 – probably the only time that the affairs of a minister's spouse have taken precedence over the affairs of state.

Clearly, Jowell would have been very aware of the restrictions on trading with Iran.

All the more curious then when one weekend in February 2003, Mills took three businessmen from Aurigny Air in the Channel Islands to Tehran to put a deal to the Iranians to operate aircraft in and out of Iran from Dubai. At a time when Ms Jowell was urging the country to war with Iraq in support of our US allies, her husband was trying to make a fast buck in the far more dangerous adjacent country by undermining the foreign policy of that very same ally.

In 2003, it was revealed he was involved in an unsuccessful deal for Iranian airline Mahan Air to buy a fleet of BAe 146 aircraft from British Aerospace. He said the sale did not go through and that he was not granted any preferential treatment. However, Foreign Office Minister Baroness Symons gave advice to Mills on the political climate surrounding the project.

# And
# Also. . .

# Coining It

Peter Cuthbertson

Disgraced ministers have returned to office following scandals before New Labour came to power. But it took Tony Blair to truly pioneer the technique of bringing back ministers who resigned over sleaze only to lose the *same* minister to sleaze once again. This cavalier attitude to using character references when re-hiring has not only guaranteed further scandals and abuse of office by unreformed ministers such as David Blunkett and Peter Mandelson, but has ensured the scandal of these ministers earning enough severance pay in a short space of time to qualify as a second income.

Owing to a system that began in 1991, Cabinet Ministers are entitled to a quarter of their annual incomes as severance pay when they resign. It is unlikely that this means of guarding against retiring Cabinet Ministers facing precipitous falls in income after leaving office was designed with the aim of boosting the bank balances of those who resigned multiple times in disgrace. But by doing so, David Blunkett and Peter Mandelson were able to milk the system for all it was worth.

For resigning from four different cabinet posts during New Labour's first two terms, Blunkett and Mandelson were able to split between them more than £60,000 of taxpayers' money in severance payments. Mandelson's first resignation over the home loans scandal brought a payoff off at least £11,000 – and Stephen Byers, his successor as Trade and Industry Secretary, confirmed the final figure could be as much as £15,412. His swift return to office, and then the accompanying resignation over the Hinduja passports scandal, netted Mandelson a further £12,129.

David Blunkett did even better for himself, taking £18,725 for his December 2004 resignation for speeding up the visa application for his lover's foreign nanny, and netting another £18,725 just 11 months later when forced to resign from his new position after his links to the firm DNA Bioscience.

Even in the (brief) intervening period before Blair brought him back as Work and Pensions Secretary, Blunkett was to live at the taxpayers' considerable expense in the

£3 million Belgravia mansion intended for the use of *sitting* Cabinet Ministers. The annual rent for such a home, owned legitimately by any private citizen, would be about £150,000 – plus an extra £50,000 in taxes. David Blunkett was paying neither.

In case anyone thought this scandalous abuse of taxpayers' funds was over, it has to be recalled that in 2004 Tony Blair returned Peter Mandelson to office an incredible third time, sending him to Brussels to be Britain's EU Commissioner, responsible for Europe's trade policy. Along with all the perks Eurocrats receive at all levels, Peter Mandelson can look forward to his gold-plated EU pension after he leaves office – even if for once, this time, he manages to do so legitimately.

*www.concom.blogspot.com*

# Constituencies for Coronets

Paul Linford

Long before it was alleged that Tony Blair had handed out seats in the House of Lords in return for loans to the Labour Party or help in establishing his flagship city academies the whiter-than-white one was busy abusing the honours system for political purposes. The business of becoming a Labour peer under Blair has often had less to do with merit and more to do with whether you have a safe Commons seat available for one of his favourites.

It doesn't always work. Before the 1997 election, Blair persuaded the long-serving Dudley MP Sir John Gilbert to step down, on the promise of being made a minister in the Lords, to create a vacancy for his former flatmate and best chum Charlie Falconer.

Unfortunately for him, Falconer bombed at the selection meeting when it emerged that he sent his children to private school, and the PM eventually had to make him a peer too in order to get him into the Government.

Blair was also determined to find a seat for the Tory defector Alan Howarth, who had assumed an importance as a symbol of New Labour's "big tent" style of politics, out of all proportion to his ability.

The veteran Newport East MP Roy Hughes was duly prevailed upon to stand down in his favour, shortly afterwards re-emerging as Lord Islwyn despite having enjoyed a Commons career of stultifying mediocrity.

More recently, in 2001, Blair set about trying to find a way of getting the head of his policy unit, David Miliband, into the Commons, as a necessary precursor to bringing him into the Cabinet.

Eventually the veteran South Shields MP and former Cabinet Minister Dr David Clark agreed to fall on his sword, being rewarded with both a peerage and the chairmanship of the Forestry Commission.

Blair has also attempted to use the honours system as a means of repaying political debts and patching up broken promises.

Back in 1995, he famously persuaded the then Labour Chief Whip, Derek Foster, to stand down, promising him a Cabinet job when Labour returned to Government with the words "and I don't mean a tiddler like Transport". Foster was in fact given a junior ministerial role so menial he resigned it after 48 hours, whereupon he was offered both a peerage and the chairmanship of the soon-to-be-created North-East Development Agency as a consolation prize. To his credit, Foster stood firm before finally taking ermine in 2005.

*www.paullinford.blogspot.com*

# Anyone Got a Match?

Jenny Geddes

In 1997 Labour promised Scotland a "Bonfire of the Quangos". Well, they not only took the piss but poured it over said bonfire. In June 2005 it was revealed the Labour (and LibDem) Executive spent £1.68 billion a year more on quangos than four years previously. Staff numbers had increased by 7,000 in the last year.

And why not? It's a nice earner for Labour hacks.

Take Norman Murray, former Labour convenor of COSLA, for example. He was appointed in 2002 to the Scottish Ambulance Service board at £7,305 a year.

Leading Lanarkshire Labour councillor Harry McGuigan was appointed a member of the Scottish Children's Reporter Administration board.

Former Edinburgh council leader Lesley Hinds and Donald Anderson, the current one, are members of the Health Education Board for Scotland and VisitScotland respectively.

Brian Cavanagh, formerly of Edinburgh council, is the £36,505-a-year chairman of Lothian NHS Board. Mr Cavanagh was discovered allowing Labour politicians to vet Health Board press releases to save political embarrassment.

Formerly of Strathclyde Council, John Mullin was Chairman of NHS Argyll and Clyde. It was so badly run financially that the Executive had to scrap it entirely and split it up between NHS Highland and NHS Greater Glasgow.

Listed as Shettleston Labour members, Professor Alan Alexander and wife Morag did quite well out of our largesse. In 2002 Alan became Chairman of Scottish Water at £70,000 a year for three-and-a-half-days a week. Morag was less lucky only collecting £21,000 a year for her part-time role as convener of the Scottish Social Services Council. Alan has since resigned, having differences of opinion with the Labour-LibDem Executive.

Former Lothian Councillor William Roe couldn't believe his luck when he became Chairman of Highlands & Islands Enterprise since the quango had given his

Hebridean software company Mysterian a support package of almost £200,000. Several weeks later it went into administration.

In June 2004 Willie Haughey, who donated hundreds of thousands to Labour, was appointed chairman of Scottish Enterprise Glasgow. In April 2005 Jack McConnell met Haughey to discuss compensation because the M74 would pass through Haughey's property. Initial compensation of £7.4 million rose to £16.5 million. And just this March it was reported that the quango Haughey chairs awarded his company nearly £1 million in addition to the above compensation. No wonder Haughey's gifts to Labour had topped £1 million. We were paying.

# Lanarkshire Labour Mafia

Jenny Geddes

Was John Reid smoking something when he claimed the 85 pence worth of cannabis found in his house was not connected to him? Course it was mate. It was in your house. OK, you may have not been partaking or even know who was partaking but it got in there somehow.

Considering the company Dr Reid and Lanarkshire Labour keeps, maybe the police should be furthering their inquiries. In October 2002 the Lanarkshire Labour party held a Red Rose Fundraising Dinner. One of the guests was a notorious drug baron called Justin McAlroy. In September 2005 John Reid's son married the daughter of Ronnie Campbell – a west of Scotland gangland figure. Heaven knows how Labour gets away with having such links but don't expect Strathclyde Police to do a Met and start taking the law more seriously.

Maybe they were policing some of the interminable marches by certain Irish organisations that blight the area or investigating the links between Ulster paramilitaries and organised crime.

Sectarianism in the Labour Party was something the former Labour First Minister Henry McLeish complained about in March 2002 when he said that he had been marked out because he wasn't Protestant, Catholic, hadn't gone to Glasgow University and wasn't part of the Lanarkshire Labour mafia.

In October 2002 First Minster Jack McConnell confirmed this sectarianism in Lanarkshire Labour when he admitted hearing some Labour members say, "You cannot vote for him, his wife is called Bridget," while others warned that McConnell should not be backed because he was "a Proddie".

Since then he went on a public crusade against Scotland's "shame" by publicly lambasting myriad organisations for not doing enough. This resulted in criticism from one football chairman, the Orange Lodge saying it was being unfairly singled out, and the unprecedented remarks of the Catholic Church who said the issue was being overblown.

The response has seen some positive moves by both Rangers and Celtic Football Clubs and march organisers signing a joint declaration to behave. The Catholic Church even gave the Orange Order's Grand Master a column in the Scottish Catholic Observer – but more to spite McConnell than because of him.

However, one organisation has been strangely silent on how it would tackle the admitted sectarianism within its ranks. You've guessed it. The Labour Party.

# The Scottish Dome

Jenny Geddes

I f we wrote the whole saga of the Holyrood project it would need a new book. But there are notable incidents pointing to Labour's sleazy attitude for letting an initial estimate balloon from £50 million to over £400 million.

In March 1998 the Spanish architect Enric Miralles was shortlisted for the Scottish Parliament contract. Nothing odd about that you would think. However, he had been rejected by the then project manager Bill Armstrong. Armstrong put him 44th out of 70 and if he'd known Miralles had no UK insurance cover he would have been number 70.

So who did shortlist him? The finger points at Scottish Secretary Donald Dewar for wanting a Catalan to dish the Nats. Armstrong eventually resigned over the political interference.

In January 1999 Bovis Lend Lease got the contract to build the Parliament. This was despite being initially eliminated from the tender process for being too expensive.

Since no Parliament had even been elected this mysterious reinstatement can only have been done by the Labour-run Scottish Office. Was it coincidence that McAlpine had been rejected despite having the lowest bid and because they had been donors to the Conservative Party?

Is it also coincidence that in May 2001 Robin Young, former non-executive director of Bovis, was appointed permanent secretary at the DTI? Weren't Bovis earning enough from an open-ended contract that made a mockery of the £50 million estimate?

By June 1999 there were fresh-faced MSPs ready to vote on handing control of the project to the Parliament from the Executive. It passed by three votes. It transpired later that extra costs on risk assessment were not disclosed by Executive Ministers during the debate. The then Finance Minister was one Jack McConnell – present First Minister.

Then we have a construction firm, O'Rourke Group, revealed in July 2002 as earning £36m for a Scottish Parliament building contract given by Bovis. The O'Rourke Group is a donor to the Labour Party.

But it still doesn't end there. In January 2005 Sarah Davidson, once adviser to former Scottish secretary Helen Liddell, landed £75,000 a year to enforce McConnell's smoking ban. The new job was never advertised.

What has this to do with Holyrood? She was the civil servant who presided over a £200m rise in the cost of Holyrood before taking a six-month sabbatical to travel round the world.

# Mr Blunkett's Many Homes

Grant Morrison

When David Blunkett stood up to make his maiden speech in 1987 few can have guessed how literally he would take himself. He made clear he felt Government should support "… their tenants to ensure that together they are able to repair the desperate housing stock currently existing in many of our major areas". Mr Blunkett was obviously so keen to help that when he entered Government he took the first opportunity to subsidise the renovations to a rundown house in Wimbledon, owned by one "David Blunkett". Whilst Mr Blunkett lived in his grace-and-favour flat in Belgravia, he was receiving £700 a month in rent for his Wimbledon house, which he was using to renovate the property. Mr Blunkett felt it unnecessary to declare the extra income in the Register of Members' Interests although the rules stated that any "significant" income should be declared.

During his maiden speech Mr Blunkett also made his thoughts clear on property ownership, saying, "Talk of a property or share or capital owning democracy is an insult to the people of Sheffield Brightside." True to his word Mr Blunkett has done much over the years to avoid paying a mortgage. More than a year after his (second) resignation from the Cabinet Mr Blunkett was still living rent free in his £3million 'dis'-grace-and-favour flat in Belgravia. Mr Blunkett felt it would be uncivilised for us to ask him to move out any faster.

Luckily, Mr Blunkett had somewhere quieter to muse over his long-awaited move from Belgravia. On the Chatsworth estate is his taxpayer-subsidised cottage that we must assume is essential to his job as a backbench MP. Perhaps the 15-mile journey from Chatsworth to Mr Blunkett's Sheffield Brightside home is further than an old socialist can be expected to travel after a hard day relaxing on one of the country's grandest estates at the taxpayers' expense.

However, it's nice to know that despite his long and highly subsidised journey up the property ladder Mr Blunkett still hasn't forgotten the people of Sheffield

Brightside. Whilst writing to voice concerns over a proposed development near his Sheffield house there was an unfortunate mix-up and rather than being written on standard notepaper his objections were written and sent on much 'weightier' official notepaper – well, after all, one day he might want to visit there again and who knows maybe even stay the night.

But as they say, "Every cloud has a silver lining", and as we sit here and stare into the black hole that is the Government finances and wonder how we'll afford our own retirements we, the great British public, have at least one thing to be grateful for. Mr Blunkett won't be making another maiden speech.

# Luvved up – Gordon on Film

Damon Lambert

Despite his macho and unnecessary workaholism, many will be surprised to know that official portraits state that the Chancellor has interests, and one of them is film. Wilf Stevenson, one of his university mates was a long-term director of the British Film Institute. Indeed, the first party Gordon Brown held at Number 11 was for movie-makers. Handed out to those long time Labour-loving luvvies with the cheese straws was the Bucks fizz of taxpayers' cash, in the form of tax reliefs. The Cassandras at the Treasury had predicted the reliefs would be used to avoid tax, just like the loopholes Brown spent the pre-1997 years lecturing the public that Labour would close. And don't forget this was in addition to Lottery and licence fee monies.

The cost of these tax incentives was estimated to be £15 million. Due to the predicted avoidance, it turned out to be £540 million per year, or about 0.5p off the tax rate for all corporates. This 'boost' to UK Film has not worked. The number of British films fell from 80 in 1997 to less than 40 in 2005 and British film exports actually dropped. A number of co-produced films have arisen to take benefit of these schemes. In 2005 there were 91 of these, only 15 of which were UK-produced. The logical thing would therefore be to abolish the reliefs. Usually New Labour never loses a chance to slam UK business for what Brown paints as tax avoidance. No chance. In 2005, in the week prior to the dissolution of Parliament just before the general election, the Government insisted on extending the reliefs, ramming the clauses through Parliament in an incredibly short Finance Bill debate that had not a single contribution from a Labour backbencher. Still, it kept a film industry, not desperately fond of Iraq wars, content. Whilst incompetence can never be ruled out when Red Dawn Primarolo is in the mix, this has all the hallmarks of government that lectures everyone else on the morality of paying tax, permitting avoidance as long as it benefits its artistic chums.

*Taxcutter, www.taxcutter.blogspot.com*

# Kinnock and the EU Whistle-blowers

Michael Wood

How could we write a book on fraud and corruption without mentioning the European Union? Whether it's agricultural payments for olive fields larger than the region that they're supposed to be in, or structural funds for motorways that stop in the middle of nowhere, you might think that there's little that even Labour politicians could teach Brussels about sleaze. You might think that, but you should know better.

Every now and again, even the EU realises that things have gone too far – that it's time that something was done to clean up the act. When those times come, you can rely on Labour to defend the status quo.

In December 1998 – back when Tony Blair was still a "pretty straight sort of guy" and Peter Mandelson was resigning for the first time – Paul van Buitenen, an assistant auditor in the European Commission, blew the whistle on widespread financial irregularities and mismanagement within the Commission. For this service, he was suspended on half pay pending disciplinary action.

Labour's reaction was swift. The leader of the Socialist MEPs, Pauline Green, supported all the Commissioners named in Mr van Buitenen's report and opposed motions calling for them to resign. The photos of Neil Kinnock thanking Mrs Green, after Labour votes ensured a majority in favour of the Commissioners staying in post, were soon seen around Europe.

Of course Labour's efforts to protect the corrupt Commissioners could only be successful for so long. In March 1999, the Commission became the first in history to be forced to resign and so a new Commission was nominated.

As if to prove that EU politicians do have a sense of humour, the new Commission President announced that the man he was putting in charge of stamping out sleaze was Neil Kinnock. Kinnock – one of the four 'resigning' Commissioners who kept their jobs – was not implicated in van Buitenen's allegations. However, any hope that anyone might have had that he would tackle EU fraud was soon to be proven misplaced.

One of the areas that Mr van Buitenen had identified as being riddled with fraud and nepotism was Eurostat – the Commission's statistical office – but it soon became clear that van Buitenen's allegations were only the tip of the iceberg. In January 2001, Dorte Schmidt Brown, a head of unit in Eurostat, wrote to Neil Kinnock with concerns about suspicious contracts worth millions. Unfortunately for Mrs Schmidt Brown, Commissioner Kinnock's response was inaction – leaving her victim to a campaign of threats and harassment, resulting in a nervous breakdown. Later, Mr Kinnock was forced to publicly apologise to her. Like other EU whistle-blowers who came forward, Mrs Schmidt Brown's career was over.

On the other hand, inaction would probably have been better than the "reward" that Marta Andreasen, the first qualified accountant to be employed as the Commission's chief accountant, received when she complained about the EU's "Enron-style bookkeeping". Initially suspended by Neil Kinnock and barred from all Commission buildings, she has now been sacked without pay – even though internal Commission documents have largely supported her claims.

Jules Muis, the Commission's senior auditor, had written to his boss – Neil Kinnock – warning him that Mrs Andreasen's claims were "factually and substantively correct". He has since resigned, complaining that the Commission prevented him from investigating fraud and that they took "no responsibility for whether the accounts are right in the end".

If only as much energy was put into investigating corruption as was put into victimising those brave enough to uncover it.

# Transforming Government

Jonathan Sheppard

If there is one area of life where Labour has done most damage it is the overt politicisation of all aspects of everyday life. As a schoolboy you were taught that the Civil Service, as with other key jobs, should be impartial and neutral. Under New Labour there has been an onslaught of political appointments in an effort to ensure that anything New Labour wants, New Labour gets.

This politicisation was most apparent during the recent vote on terror detention plans. Police forces became embroiled in politics with Chiefs of Police actively lobbying politicians in favour of a limit of 90 days for detaining terror suspects. Given that every Chief Constable was well aware that their job would be up for re-election, can it be right for our Chiefs of Police to be involved in lobbying for Government policy? How can their position be then tenable if there is a change of Government and a change in policy? It can't be, and that is why these kinds of position have to maintain their political neutrality.

From political appointments to non-elected quangos, to Chiefs of Police lobbying on behalf of Government policy, right through to an unprecedented increase in the number of Special Advisors at the heart of Government who have a remit no one could have imagined a few years previously, New Labour has indeed transformed Government, but, unfortunately, for the worse.

*Tory Radio, www.toryradio.com*

# Fooling Some of the People

Chris Palmer

When you're stuck for something new to announce, why not re-announce something you've already released and pretend it's something new? No one will notice – and while you're at it, fiddle the facts just for added effect. This is the maxim which the Chancellor of the Exchequer and successive New Labour Education and Health Secretaries have lived by for the past nine years.

This Labour Government treats the electorate and its own voters with complete contempt, believing them all to be gullible, stupid fools.

Famously, between 1998 and 2000, David Blunkett (then Education Secretary) announced every year that the Education budget would increase by an "extra £19 billion", where in actual fact, this £19 billion was really far, far less. However, not content with the magical conversion of £9.7 billion into £19 billion. How so, you ask? Nick Davies of the *Guardian* explains: "So where is the £19 billion? Maybe it is already in the schools and we have simply failed to observe it. Maybe it is on its way down the pipeline and will arrive any week now. Or maybe it never existed. Maybe the truth is that Mr Blunkett's £19bn is largely composed of magical money, literally billions of pounds which have been conjured out of thin air by trickery – double-counting, treble-counting, several bookkeeping manoeuvres and a steady stream of fundamentally misleading public statements. Watch closely and you can see the conjuror at work. The first trick is the biggest."

Ever since the birth of inflation, government departments have been increasing their spending each year. When Mr Blunkett made his grand announcement in July 1998, he was reporting the results for education of Gordon Brown's comprehensive spending review, which had laid down a budget for every Whitehall department for each of the final three years of the parliament. The existing budget for UK education, for 1998/9, was £38.3 billion. As a result of the review, Mr Blunkett was able to announce that this would rise, in 1999, by £3 billion; in 2000, by £3.5 billion; and finally, in 2001/2, by £3.2 billion. That was all he announced. But, of course that adds up to only £9.7 billion. Where was the rest of the £19 billion? The answer is that it does not exist. Contrary to Mr Blunkett's description of his £19 billion as "real", nearly half of it is manufactured by a single bookkeeping trick. It works like this. You take the increase for the first year and you say, "Well, if I pay this in the first year, it will become a permanent part of the budget, so I will still be paying it in subsequent years when I make further annual increases, so I should carry on counting it as an increase each year." This is not the way that any British government has previously accounted for its budgets. Carl Emmerson of the Institute for Fiscal Studies says it is "misleading"; David Heald, professor of accountancy at Aberdeen university and adviser to the treasury select committee, says it is "confusing" and "unprecedented". But, for Mr Blunkett, the result was simply excellent. In year one, he had a rise of £3 billion. In year two, he had a rise of £3.5 billion but he added in the £3 billion which he would still be paying from year one and called it a rise of £6.5 billion. Then he came to year three, when he had a rise of £3.2 billion, but he added in the £6.5 billion which he had already committed to the budget in the first two years and called it a rise of £9.7 billion. Then he stood back and added the whole lot up – £3 billion plus £6.5 billion plus £9.7 billion. A £19.2 billion bonanza.

Clear? Mr Blunkett and his ministers continued to indulge repeatedly in another kind of press trickery. They recycled money through a sequence of different announcements, each time pretending that they were unveiling brand new spending when, in truth, they were simply delivering old money in new clothes.

David Blunkett later moved on to become Home Secretary where he continued to concoct schemes with the same old set of tricks, with multiple releases to the press on the same topic, that attempted to portray Home Office inaction as progress. However, we all know now, that due to his deception and gross incompetence, much of the blame over the 1,000 foreign prisoners debacle can be placed at his door.

*Political Crossroads, www.politicalcrossroads.blogspot.com*

# Psychological Flaws

Paul Linford

"Your enemies are the people who sit behind you. Those in front are merely your opponents." Never was the old saying about the nature of politics more true than in the case of New Labour.

Under Tony Blair and his spin twins Peter Mandelson and Alastair Campbell, the practice of smearing one's own side was developed into a fine art.

The earliest victim was Dr David Clark. Appointed public services minister in 1997, stories soon appeared that he was spending a fortune jetting round the world looking at other countries' freedom of information legislation.

Then, in October 1997, the political editor of Clark's local paper, the *Newcastle Journal*, was startled to hear a Downing Street spin doctor tell him down the phone that Clark had "lost it" and would be sacked in the next reshuffle.

The aim of all this was twofold. First, Clark had to be got rid of because he had made the mistake of assuming Labour intended to act on its pre-election promise to bring in a wide-ranging freedom of information act, as opposed to the damp squib that finally emerged.

Second, as Paddy Ashdown's memoirs later made clear, Blair was at this time attempting to create two Cabinet vacancies to enable him to bring in Liberal Democrats, and Clark was one of those deemed dispensable.

In the event Clark survived another nine months, but he was not the only North-East MP who found himself on the wrong end of Blair's spin machine.

A couple of years later, the late Mo Mowlam, who had embarrassed Blair by earning a standing ovation during his conference speech, decided to quit politics after unnamed Labour sources openly questioned her sanity.

The most famous internecine New Labour smear of all, though, came in an interview with the *Observer*'s Andrew Rawnsley in 1998.

Rawnsley reported that someone "with an extremely good claim to know the mind of the Prime Minister" had described the Chancellor to him as "psychologically flawed".

Quite properly, Rawnsley has always refused to reveal his source, but Messrs Campbell and Mandelson head a shortlist of two.

With friends like those, New Labour has never been in need of enemies.

*www.paullinford.blogspot.com*

# Blairways Holidays – Even Cheaper Than Chips...

Steve Garrett

O ver the entire period of Blair's premiership, through that crisis, this reshuffle, those international tensions, that tsunami and the war, one activity has remained solidly unaffected within the Blair household. Nothing but nothing can shift the resolve of 'Team Blair' to get away from it all and have a really good time – preferably at someone else's expense. It is of course, the annual Blair holiday (or in the case of Team Blair, annual holidays – plural). Tone, Cherie, the kids and invited friends have made it their number one family priority to have a few months away every year – the more exotic, the better. Their number two priority seems to be to try to get someone else to pick up the tab.

They appear to have been entirely successful in both aims.

Crinkly warbler Sir Cliff Richard and former Italian PM Silvio Berlusconi have more than healthy Mediterranean tans, a mouthful of capped teeth and creative hairstyles in common. They both own rather nice exotic holiday homes in sexy locations. Add the odd minor European nobleman with the essential chateau or Tuscan villa, some big-shot city moneyman's exotic condo and you have Team Blair's very own, very private, very exclusive holiday brochure from which they choose. Hmmm, that's handy.

Not for Tony and Cherie the bother of searching the internet for bargain basement holiday deals. Not for them the hassle of queuing, pushing and shoving through passport control, waiting for luggage still somewhere over the Atlantic, arguing with a jobsworth in a peak cap and wondering whether the Latin taxi driver's car actually has any brakes under the bonnet…. Why? Because they have enlisted the help of the Queen's Flight to ease their way to their exclusive holiday destination. Hmmm, how sweet.

So, in short, it's win-win for the Blairs on their world tour. They fly for free, we pick up the tab. They stay for free, courtesy of one the long line of apparently willing millionaires and their holiday homes.

When it comes to 'front', Team Blair seem to know no boundaries. When challenged about the apparent readiness to accept free holidays and utilise the Queen's Flight to get them there, Tony Blair always makes a point of giving a donation to some charity or other. He sees it as a sort of supposedly noble justification for all the special treatment and holiday favours he calls in. How much is donated – Blair presumably has set the figure, but how does he work it out? Is a tenner enough, or would a monkey or even a pony suffice? Hmmm, Gordon, lend us your calculator will you?

A month or two ago, after much pushing, Downing Street was forced to publish the actual real cost to the taxpayer of a Team Blair holiday trip to Sharm el Sheikh in Egypt. The amount came to well over £25,000 to the taxpayer… Did Tony's charitable donation dig that deep in his pocket? I doubt it. What a truly wondrous system Team Blair have invented for themselves. They blag a freebie holiday, they get the Queen's Flight to drop them off and pick them up, then Blair decides how much he should donate in lieu! Hmmm, how convenient.

Would it work for us? Could we get the Queen's Flight to drop us off in our holiday destination in Spain? Could we blag a few weeks at some plutocrat's Caribbean pad?

Talking of Cliff, this curious piece appeared on Popbitch in April 2006: "Friends of Sir Cliff Richard are claiming that Sir Cliff was far from happy with Tony and Cherie borrowing his house in Barbados. The first time he lent them his home, the singer was apparently disappointed that they didn't offer anything. When the Blairs asked again, Sir Cliff grudgingly said yes, but insisted on an arrangement where the PM would make an appropriate donation to Cliff's favourite charity. Some months later, the charity's accountants were asked about the payment. They confirmed a donation had been made as requested. But how much did the Blairs decide to pay? Cliff's friends are putting it about that the amount the PM thought was appropriate to rent a luxury villa in Barbados for over two weeks... was about the cost of a meal for two in a London restaurant."

So, they paid about £200 quid for a three-week holiday. Obviously Cherie was writing the cheque.

I know Blair has been cleared of improper conduct regarding his holiday arrangements – but that still doesn't stop me thinking that these very rich and very well connected celebs, foreign politicians and mega-rich moneymen hosts would perhaps expect a favour or two in return for their hospitality?

'Back scratching' is, after all, an entirely human condition.

Perhaps the Blairs should take a leaf out of a previous Labour Prime Minister's more modest and less controversial holiday arrangements. I've heard the Scilly Islands just off the coast of Cornwall are very nice at this time of year…

*www.wakinghereward.blogspot.com*

# Spin Doctors Double Under Labour
Phil Taylor

Pretty much as soon as New Labour got into power it started undermining the impartiality of the Civil Service and diverting government funds to special advisers who were essentially Labour stooges paid by the State.

As early as October 2001 John Prescott gave the following answer in Parliament: "I can confirm that there are 81 special advisers... Indeed, I can confirm that the number of special advisers has increased from 38 – the number in post when we first came to office."

By July 2003 Downing Street had to admit that taxpayers had spent £5.4 million on special advisers in the 2002-03 tax year, more than double the amount spent in Labour's first year in power.

In February 2004 Tony Blair was criticised by the outgoing Commissioner on Standards in Public Life for failing to curb the power of these unelected special advisers. Sir Nigel Wicks was reported to have said that Mr Blair's reluctance to limit the influence of politically appointed spin doctors could further erode the public's trust in government.

The Government refused to accept the committee's proposal that special advisers should be defined as a category of government servant distinct from the Civil Service; that Parliament should set a limit on their number; and that Parliament should approve the granting of executive powers to people like Blair's chief of staff, Jonathan Powell, and his director of communications David Hill, who succeeded Alastair Campbell.

One of the scandals of the whole special advisor system is that they are allowed to bunk off at election time and work for their political masters at taxpayers' expense.

Special advisers are basically temporary civil servants who are exempt from the normal rules of civil service impartiality. Most are Labour activists. Under the terms of their contract, advisers who resign at election time are entitled to three months to six months' pay. Subsequently, if they are reappointed after the election they can pick up where they left off, having been paid by the state without interruption. Their "volunteering" is paid for by the state.

In the run-up to the last general election Andrew Tyrie, a Tory Treasury spokesman, said, "When the election is called, hordes of Labour advisers, most of whom have been doing nothing for months except work for the re-election of Labour, are going to descend on Labour HQ. The numbers are now so large that there is a de facto Labour Party campaign team working within Whitehall at the taxpayers' expense."

Nice work if you can get it.

# STOP PRESS

Just when you thought it couldn't get any worse . . .

## Cherie Blair's £1,200-a-Minute Fee

Ellee Seymour

With Labour's popularity sinking to an all-time low since 1992 and Conservatives storming ahead with an eight-point lead, Cherie Blair quite clearly had her priorities set out – cashing in on a lucrative speaking engagement in Dubai to boost her bank account.

Public criticism of the high fees she demands has done nothing to deter her from exploiting her privileged position in pursuit of even greater wealth. In the past she has also been criticised for using her Downing Street flat for business meetings at the taxpayers' expense.

However, on 13th May 2006 she excelled herself by earning £24,000 for a 20-minute lecture – that is £1,200 a minute – to students from the American University of Dubai.

Incredibly, her lecture was held on the same day that Mrs Blair was reported in *The Times* as saying that most of her foreign speaking engagements were unpaid. She insisted that she did not receive fees for talks she made during a recent trip to Pakistan stating quite firmly: "I do these things all the time and I don't get paid for them".

But it transpired that Mrs Blair's Dubai visit had been booked through an American agency for £24,000. On top of that she was given £6,500 first-class flights from Heathrow and £800-a-night luxury five-star suites, bringing the true cost of her visit nearer to £32,000. She was joined by two British protection officers and her agent.

Although the visit was advertised as promoting Cherie Booth QC, she was introduced as somebody with outspoken views who had the ability to multi-task as a wife, mother and professional, a figure worthy of public attention in her own right.

Her brief speech included telling the mainly Arabic audience about the need to promote greater equality and utilise the skills of women. It was never sensational and failed to be outspoken.

But it is not just cashing in on speeches as the Prime Minister's wife that has led to Mrs Blair being accused of abusing her position, she has also been criticised for using her Downing Street flat to hold meetings with clients in her legal capacity as a barrister and QC at the taxpayers' expense.

According to *The Lawyer* magazine, she held some consultations at home as part of her work as an employment law specialist at Matrix Chambers.

The Blairs occupy an extended family flat above Nos 11 and 12 Downing Street, which is paid for by the taxpayer.

It first emerged that Mrs Blair was holding business meetings at No 11 when she was working on the case surrounding the collapsed BCCI bank for her former chambers, 4-5 Gray's Inn Square.

She faced censure from critics who said the property was funded by the taxpayer and should not be used for business purposes.

Mrs Blair was criticised for hosting work meetings in Downing Street by the Criminal Law Solicitors' Association in August 2000.

Franklin Sinclair, its chairman, said at the time: "You have to ask who is paying for the conference and its administration. She should use her chambers like everyone else."

Mrs Blair has maintained her legal practice despite being the Prime Minister's wife. However, her legal role has brought her into conflict with the Government, particularly over her speciality of employment law and human rights.

*Ellee Seymour, www.elleeseymour.blogspot.com*

# Useful Links

| | |
|---|---|
| New Labour Sleaze | **www.newlaboursleaze.com** |
| New Labour Unplugged | **www.newlabourunplugged.com** |
| Labour Sleaze | **www.laboursleaze.com** |
| Backing Blair | **www.backingblair.co.uk** |
| Blair Watch | **www.blairwatch.co.uk** |

I'M A PRETTY STRAIGHT SORT OF GUY